AF575650

AVIATION

C-17 Globemaster III

McDonnell Douglas / Boeing's Military Transport

KEN NEUBECK

Library of Congress Control Number: 2020952535

Type set in Impact/Minion Pro/Univers LT Std

ISBN: 978-0-7643-6288-0
Printed in India

Published by Schiffer Publishing, Ltd.
4880 Lower Valley Road
Atglen, PA 19310
Phone: (610) 593-1777; Fax: (610) 593-2002
Email: Info@schifferbooks.com
Web: www.schifferbooks.com

Acknowledgments

The author has gained knowledge on the C-17 aircraft through his work with three different subcontractors that either had bid or have had products incorporated on the aircraft.

The author thanks those who contributed photos to the book, including John Gourley, McDonnell Douglas archive photos, Boeing, and the US Air Force. The author wants to especially thank Oscar Hollenbeck and the airport staff at Stewart Airport for their help in providing onboard access to C-17 aircraft based at the airport. In addition, the author wishes to thank Audrey Cohen and the Epoch 5 public relations staff, as well as Shelley LaRose Arken and the staff of Long Island MacArthur airport for their help in providing access to the C-17 support aircraft during the USAF Thunderbirds team visit to Long Island.

The first C-17 aircraft, designated as T-1, makes its first flight on September 15, 1992, from the McDonnell Douglas Company facility located in Long Beach, California. *McDonnell Douglas Archives*

Abbreviations used in photo credits:
LIRAHS = Long Island Republic Airport Historical Society
USAF = United States Air Force

Contents

CHAPTER 1

Development and Production

C-17 program emblem as developed by McDonnell Douglas in 1986. *McDonnell Douglas Archives*

During the 1970s, the US Air Force (USAF) began looking for a replacement for the Lockheed C-130 transport aircraft. A proposal was developed called the Advanced Medium STOL (Short Takeoff and Landing) Transport (AMST). There were two competing designs for the proposal: the Boeing YC-14 and the McDonnell Douglas YC-15. However, the competition was canceled before a winner was selected.

The USAF then released another request for proposals for a C-X transport program in October 1980. McDonnell Douglas developed a new aircraft that was based on the YC-15 design, while Boeing bid an enlarged three-engine version of its YC-14 design. In addition, Lockheed submitted a C-5-based design and an enlarged C-141 design. In August 1981, McDonnell Douglas was chosen to build its proposed aircraft, which would be designated as the C-17.

Compared to the original YC-15 design, the new aircraft differed in having swept wings, increased size, and more-powerful engines. The increased capacity would allow the aircraft to perform the work done by the C-141, and to take over some of the duties of the Lockheed C-5 Galaxy, which would free up the C-5 fleet for outsized cargo.

However, the C-17 program was delayed while alternative designs were studied by USAF, particularly in the wake of the aging C-141 fleet. Finally, in December 1985, a full-scale development contract was awarded, with first flight initially planned for 1990. At the time, the USAF established a requirement for 210 aircraft. This number would be trimmed to 120 aircraft in 1990 by the secretary of defense.

In the late 1980s, the Long Beach, California, facility, which built MD-80 aircraft, was expanded by McDonnell Douglas for the C-17 program. Flight testing would be conducted at the runway of the adjacent Long Beach municipal airport.

Specifications

Crew: 3 (pilot, copilot, loadmaster)
Capacity: 170,900 pounds
Length: 174 feet
Wingspan: 169 feet, 9.6 inches
Height: 55 feet, 1 inch
Wing area: 3,800 feet^2
Empty weight: 283,000 pounds
Max. takeoff weight: 585,000 pounds
Fuel capacity: 35,546 US gallons
Power plant: 4 Pratt & Whitney F117-PW-100 turbofan engines; 40,440 pounds thrust each
Performance
Cruise speed: 450 knots (520 mph)
Range: 2,420 nautical miles (2,780 miles) with 157,000 pounds of payload
Ferry range: 4,300 nautical miles (4,900 miles)
Service ceiling: 45,000 feet (14,000 miles)
Takeoff run at maximum takeoff weight: 8,200 feet
Takeoff run at 395,000 pounds: 3,000 feet
Landing distance: 3,500 feet with maximum payload

This is the second YC-15 prototype, serial number 72-1876, that was made by McDonnell Douglas. After completing flight testing, this aircraft would be on display on museum row for several years at the Davis Monthan boneyard facility located in Tucson, Arizona. The four engines have been stripped from the airframe, and the cockpit windows are covered with protective covering. Remnants of the Southeast Asia (SEA) paint scheme remain on the fuselage and wings. The aircraft would be scrapped in April 2012. *Ken Neubeck*

This is the second YC-14 prototype that was manufactured by Boeing, serial number 72-1874, which competed with the YC-15 design and is shown here in the Davis Monthan boneyard. In contrast to the YC-15 four-engine design, this aircraft had only two engines. After completing flight testing in 1980, this aircraft was also put on museum row at the Davis Monthan. *Ken Neubeck*

The second YC-15 prototype, serial number 72-1876, shown here in the Davis Monthan boneyard, was different from the first YC-15 prototype since its wingspan was only 110 feet, compared to 132 feet on the first aircraft. In addition, during phase 2 of the testing, one of the four Pratt & Whitney JT8-17 engines was swapped out with a Pratt & Whitney JT8-209 engine in the number 1 nacelle position. *Ken Neubeck*

Initial static testing in 1992 showed that the C-17 wing design did not meet the design load-testing requirements, since there were cracks in the wing components. Additional money of over $100 million had to be allocated to redesign the wing. After additional testing was performed in 1993 and failed, however, it was eventually determined that the aircraft had passed the test. The aircraft would officially be designated as the Globemaster III in 1993.

Production began at the Long Beach facility in 1991 and would reach peak production rates of sixteen aircraft per year from the years 2002 through 2009. Throughout the program, there were budget overruns and other issues that threatened cutting the overall number of aircraft that were ordered for the program. It was also determined that the C-17 had only a modest improvement over the C-5A with regard to airfields outside the US, of about 1,000 airfields that were reviewed. The first C-17 squadron was declared operational by the USAF in January 1995.

In 1997, Boeing would merge with McDonnell Douglas, and the new company would continue under the Boeing name.

In July 2010, congressional testimony by the USAF stated that the service had more than enough C-17s (223 at the time), and that the US military transport fleet with the C-5A aircraft (110 at the time) would fulfill airlift needs for several years into the future. Thus, production needs for USAF would begin to wind down at this point.

Foreign contracts helped extend the production line at the Long Beach facility by fifty additional aircraft; however, with no further orders, the last C-17 (number 279) rolled off the production line in 2015. Boeing would close the C-17 buildings in Long Beach in 2015 as well and sell off the buildings over the next few years.

Although it would often be compared with the C-130, the C-17 was never considered to be a direct replacement for the Hercules. Likewise, the C-17 was meant to take over only some of the C-5A's missions. However, it has found a niche performing certain transport missions.

C-17 Globemaster III USAF Program Summary

Lot Number	Quantity	Tail Number
Test aircraft T1	1	87-0025
US Production Lot I	2	88-0265–88-0266
US Production Lot II	4	89-1189–89-1192
US Production Lot III	4	90-0532–90-0535
US Production Lot IV	4	92-3291–92-3294
US Production Lot V	6	93-0599–93-0604
US Production Lot VI	6	94-0065–94-0070
US Production Lot VII	6	95-0102–95-0107
US Production Lot VIII	8	96-0001–96-0008
US Production Lot IX	8	97-0041–97-0048
US Production Lot X	9	98-0049–98-0057
US Production Lot XI	13	99-0058–99-0064
		99-0165–99-0170
US Production Lot XII	15	00-0171–00-0185
US Production Lot XIII	12	01-0186–01-0197
US Production Lot XIV	15	02-1098–02-1112
US Production Lot XV	15	03-3113–03-3127
US Production Lot XVI	11	04-4128–04-4138
US Production Lot XVII	15	05-5139–05-5153
US Production	15	06-6154–06-6168
US Production	21	07-7169–07-7189
US Production	15	08-8189–08-8204
US Production	8	09-9205–09-9212
US Production	11	10-0213–10-0223
TOTAL (USAF)	230	

This original McDonnell Douglas YC-15 prototype, serial number 72-1875, used in the USAF transport competition, was tested at Edwards AFB in the late 1970s. This aircraft was retired by 1980 and then would be made flightworthy and used again in 1997 for further testing. After the aircraft was retired, the exterior of the aircraft, including the engine nacelles, was restored and is currently on display at the museum at Edwards AFB, California. *USAF photo by SrA Stacy Sanchez*

The T1 prototype, serial number 87-0025, was the first C-17 produced, and it arrived at Edwards AFB from the company plant in Long Beach, California, during its first flight on September 15, 1991. The crew consisted both McDonnell Douglas and USAF test personnel. *USAF*

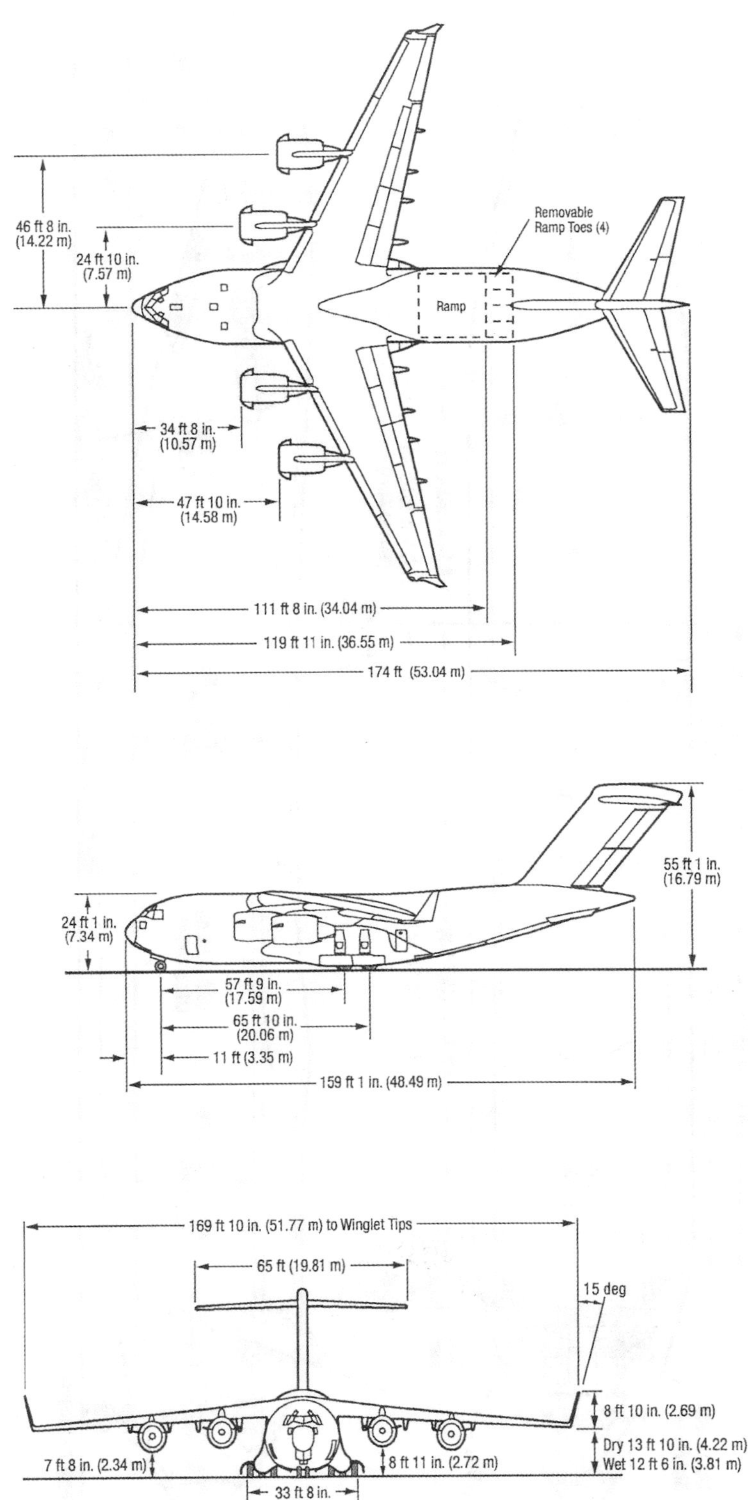

These are the detailed dimensions of the C-17 Globemaster III. *Boeing*

The C-17 Globemaster III carries forward the name of two previous Douglas piston-engine military cargo aircraft, the Douglas C-74 Globemaster and the Douglas C-124 Globemaster II. Shown here is the C-74 Globemaster. A total of fourteen C-74 aircraft were built, with eleven actually seeing service. The last aircraft was retired in 1956. *USAF*

Here is the C-124 Globemaster II in action during the Korean War. A total of 448 C-124s were built, with the last aircraft retired from the Air National Guard in 1974. *USAF*

The C-17 T-1 prototype aircraft conducting flight testing at Owens Valley, California, near Edwards AFB, on April 8, 2004. The aircraft had just undergone 200 days of modifications in Texas prior to delivery to Edwards. *USAF*

Here is the T1 aircraft flying on September 15, 2011, the twentieth anniversary of its first flight. This aircraft would fly for twenty-one years, with thousands of hours accrued for flight and ground tests. There were modifications to equipment as well as the airframe. Special tests included running the aircraft on synthetic fuel blends. *Boeing*

The T1 aircraft would be modified several times during the course of its operational history. Modifications were made to parts of the cockpit, which is shown here. *USAF photo by Jeff Fisher*

Generals Merrill McPeak and Ronald Fogelman disembark from the "Spirit of Charleston," which was the first C-17 to be delivered to the Air Force on June 14, 1993. Gen. McPeak was the chief of staff of the USAF, and Gen. Fogelman was the commander of Air Mobility Command. *USAF photo by Ken Hackman*

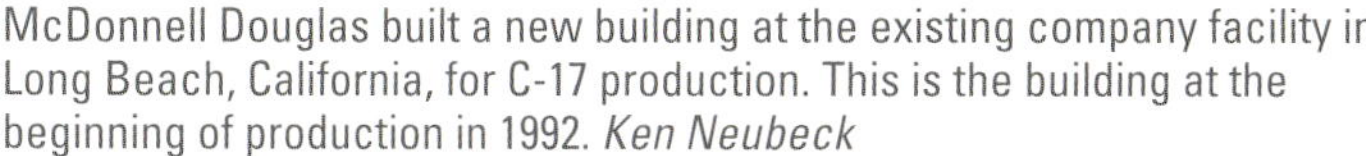
McDonnell Douglas built a new building at the existing company facility in Long Beach, California, for C-17 production. This is the building at the beginning of production in 1992. *Ken Neubeck*

This is a view of the forward fuselage section on a C-17 production aircraft that is under construction at the McDonnell facility in Long Beach. *Boeing*

The "Spirit of Charleston" flies over the Charleston base during initial flights after delivery in June 1993. Charleston would be the first operational base for the aircraft under the 437th Airlift Wing. *USAF photo by TSgt. David McLeod*

CHAPTER 2

Comparison with Other USAF Transports

There are a number of USAF military transport aircraft that were developed some years before the C-17. Besides the C-17, the USAF uses the C-130, C-141, and C-5, all of which were developed more than thirty years ago. Each transport aircraft program has presented a challenge with regard to development and deployment into operational service.

The C-5 tends to be used for extra-large and heavier cargo. However, the mere size and weight of the C-5 restrict the ability of this aircraft to land at many airports in the US, particularly if some preparations are needed to secure smaller aircraft present at these airports.

While the C-130 is more prevalent in terms of number and by being smaller, it can land at most airfields; it also has a smaller cargo capability that the other transports. This may require additional C-130s being needed when there is a large load to be carried. It all depends on what airfields are involved, what transport aircraft is readily available, and what cargo loads are involved.

In fiscal year 2009, the USAF C-17 fleet of 218 aircraft flew a total of 162,400 flight hours, which represents 42 percent of the total USAF transport fleet workload (including C-5 and C-130 aircraft). By fiscal year 2013, the number of flying hours for the C-17 fleet of 218 aircraft increased to 178,000 flight hours, representing over 53 percent of the total USAF transport fleet, with reductions in available C-5 and C-130 aircraft.

For the USAF Thunderbirds flight demonstration team, there is no assigned transport for the team, so the transport of equipment is assigned to either a C-130 or C-17, depending on availability. The C-17 is often the best choice for certain assignments because of its design. In this chapter, the different models are compared with the C-17 with regard to size and cargo capabilities.

The C-17 Globemaster III represents a general-purpose transport that can be used for certain assignments and locations that often preclude the use of other USAF transport aircraft. A total of 230 C-17 aircraft were built for the USAF, and fifty C-17 aircraft were built for foreign countries. *Ken Neubeck*

The C-141 Starlifter is powered by four jet engines and was manufactured by Lockheed, making its first flight in December 1963. A total of 285 aircraft were built, with about sixty still in service with the USAF. *USAF photo by SSgt. Tony R. Tolley*

The C-5 Galaxy is powered by four jet engines and was also manufactured by Lockheed, making its first flight in June 1968. A total of 131 aircraft were built. The aircraft had some service issues, with cracks occurring in the wings. About fifty of the C-5M version remain in service with the USAF. *USAF*

AIRCRAFT COMPARISONS

This simplified diagram shows some of the basic envelope dimension and cargo capabilities between the C-17 as compared to other existing transport aircraft such as the C-130 and C-5 aircraft. *Boeing*

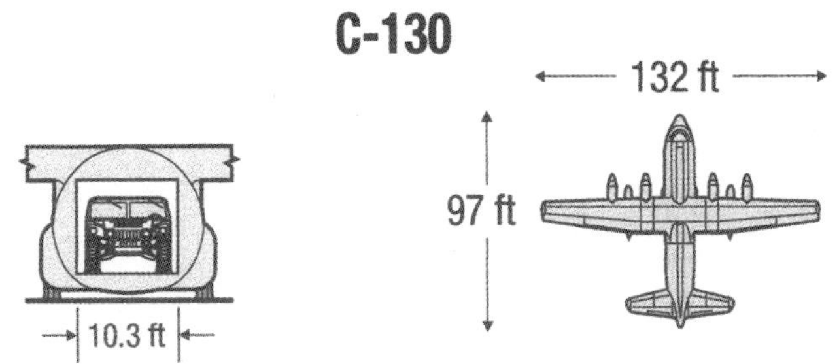

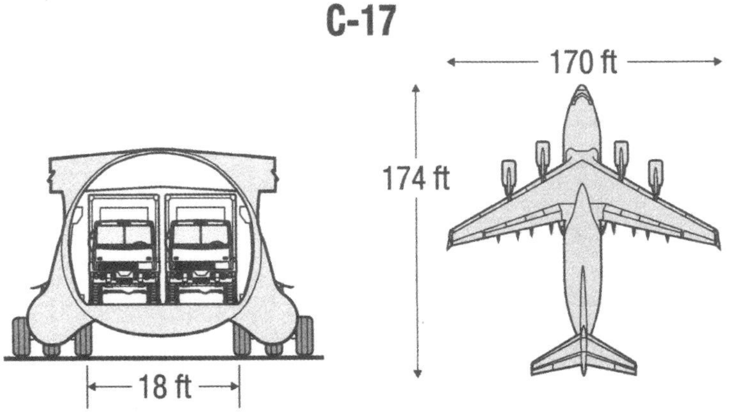

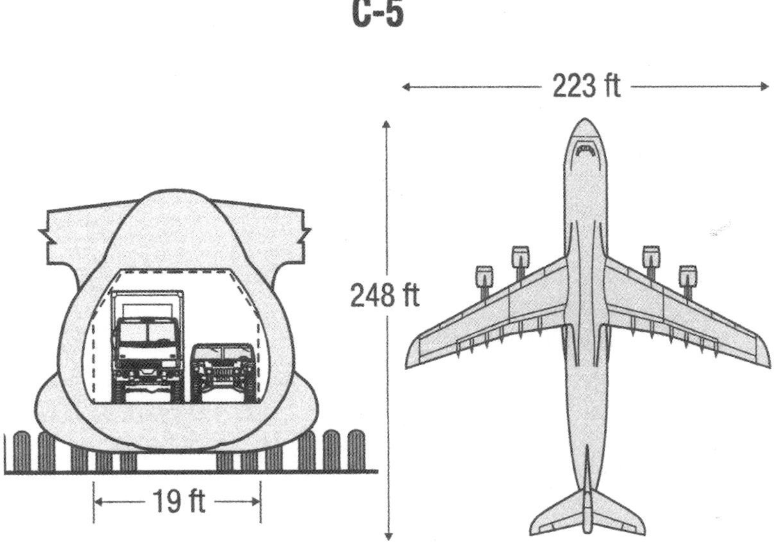

The venerable C-130 Hercules has remained in service since its first flight in August 1954, up to the present day. It is powered by four turboprop engines and is capable of carrying payloads up to 45,000 pounds, with a cargo area of 40 feet long by 10 feet wide by 9 feet high. Over 2,500 C-130 aircraft have been built, with a large number still in service today. This C-130 aircraft is conducting a drop in place at Republic Airport in Farmingdale, New York, with engines running, delivering supplies to Long Island during the aftermath of Hurricane Sandy in October 2012. *Ken Neubeck*

In addition to transport duties, the C-130 aircraft is also used in a variety of unique and different missions that continue to extend its service to the present day, making it a valuable aircraft. One current mission is firefighting service as seen in this C-130J from the Channel Island ANG from California that is landing at MacArthur Airport in Long Island, New York. This aircraft is marked with bright orange numerical markings indicating the aircraft's service in firefighting assignments in the western United States. *Ken Neubeck*

In contrast to the C-130, the C-17 is powered by four jet engines, has more cargo hold capability, and is capable of carrying up to 170,000 pounds of payload in a cargo area of 88 feet long, 18 feet wide, and 12 feet, 4 inches high. This C-17 from Travis AFB has just landed at MacArthur Airport in Long Island, New York. *Ken Neubeck*

A number of the air mobility bases in the US will operate both the C-130 and the C-17 transport aircraft. Here are C-130 aircraft that are based at Stewart ANG base in Newburgh, New York. *Ken Neubeck*

Here is a pair of C-17 aircraft out of the nine that are operating at Stewart ANG base in New York to complement the existing C-130 aircraft. *Ken Neubeck*

It is not unusual for the C-17 to be used with other USAF transport aircraft during certain events. Shown here is a C-17 from McChord AFB with a C-141 aircraft on the runway in Libreville, Gabon, in March 1991, where the two aircraft were used to evacuate US personnel in that country. *USAF photo by SSgt Andy Dunaway*

Another event in which the C-17 is regularly seen is with the USAF Thunderbirds team during the course of the yearly airshow schedule. Here are the team's maintenance personnel boarding a C-17 for the ride home to the Thunderbirds base in Las Vegas, Nevada, at the conclusion of the Jones Beach Air Show on Long Island in May 2021. The C-17 aircraft assigned is based on what aircraft is available at the time. *Ken Neubeck*

CHAPTER 3

Details

The C-17 Globemaster III is powered by four Pratt & Whitney F117-PW-100 turbofan engines, which is the military version of the commercial Pratt & Whitney PW2040 used on the Boeing 757. The engine's thrust reversers direct engine exhaust air upward and forward, reducing the chances of foreign-object damage by ingestion of runway debris, and providing enough reverse thrust to back the aircraft up on the ground while taxiing.

Unique features for the C-17 include the multiple set of main landing-gear wheel assemblies. These wheels support the weight of the aircraft on the ground, and when the aircraft is in flight, each wheel assembly rotates and turns flush with the lower fuselage of the aircraft.

For a large transport aircraft such as the C-17, there are several flight control surfaces located throughout the body of the aircraft. This includes both the leading and trailing edges of each wing, along with two-piece vertical rudder section and the horizontal tail section as well.

The C-17 is designed to handle a maximum of 170,900 pounds of cargo and to operate from runways as short as 3,500 feet and as narrow as 90 feet. In addition, the C-17 can operate from unpaved, unimproved runways.

For cargo operations, the C-17 requires a minimum crew of three: pilot, copilot, and loadmaster. The C-17 has specific geometry inside the cargo area to maximize the use of this area. The cargo floor has rollers for palletized cargo, but it can be flipped to provide a flat floor suitable for vehicles and other rolling stock. Cargo is loaded through a large aft ramp that accommodates various items such as tanks, helicopters, and trucks, and with palletized cargo.

The following pages show some of the unique details of the aircraft.

Through both static testing on the ground and flight testing, the C-17 design has evolved from the YC-15 prototype, with structural upgrades having been implemented for the aircraft to meet the required load parameters. *Ken Neubeck*

Front view of the C-17 shows the landing-gear arrangement of the nose landing-gear assembly and the main landing-gear assemblies that are used to support the massive transport aircraft. Board stairs are part of the entrance door, as seen on the left side of the aircraft. *USAF photo by Senior Airman Dennis Sloan.*

This is another view of the C-17 nose landing gear and the stairs located on the left side of the aircraft, which is typically used for pilot and loadmaster entrance to the aircraft. *Ken Neubeck*

Forward view of the nose landing-gear assembly shows the two halves of the door assemblies that are extended from the landing-gear strut. The nosewheel consists of a dual tire assembly that surrounds the strut. *John Gourley*

Closeup view of the nose landing gear and landing-gear doors. *Ken Neubeck*

The main feature of the C-17 is the fuselage area that allows for a large amount of equipment to be loaded into the aircraft. The Travis AFB-based C-17 shown here was used to support the USAF Thunderbirds aerobatic team during their May 2021 visit to the Jones Beach Air Show on Long Island, New York. *Ken Neubeck*

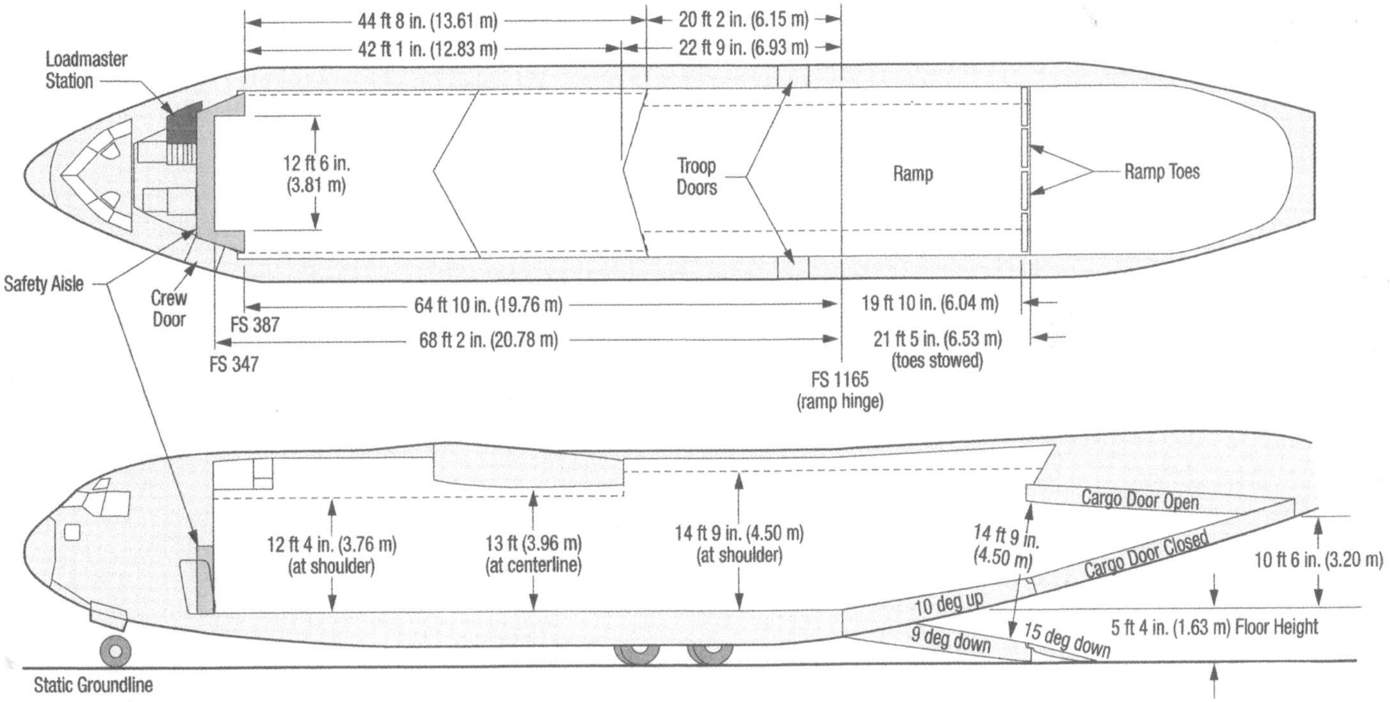

44 ft 8 in. (13.61 m)
20 ft 2 in. (6.15 m)
42 ft 1 in. (12.83 m)
22 ft 9 in. (6.93 m)
Loadmaster Station
12 ft 6 in. (3.81 m)
Troop Doors
Ramp
Ramp Toes
Safety Aisle
Crew Door
64 ft 10 in. (19.76 m)
19 ft 10 in. (6.04 m)
FS 387
68 ft 2 in. (20.78 m)
21 ft 5 in. (6.53 m) (toes stowed)
FS 347
FS 1165 (ramp hinge)
Cargo Door Open
12 ft 4 in. (3.76 m) (at shoulder)
13 ft (3.96 m) (at centerline)
14 ft 9 in. (4.50 m) (at shoulder)
14 ft 9 in. (4.50 m)
Cargo Door Closed
10 ft 6 in. (3.20 m)
10 deg up
9 deg down
15 deg down
5 ft 4 in. (1.63 m) Floor Height
Static Groundline

This diagram shows the actual dimensions of the cargo area of the C-17, along with the locations of the crew and troop doors. The cargo area has been maximized to hold large cargo items such as military vehicles and helicopters. *Boeing*

The main landing-gear assemblies are massive structures located on the lower fuselage of the C-17. Pictured here is the right-side main landing gear. *Ken Neubeck*

This is a close-up view of the left main landing-gear assembly area. Here, one of the cargo hold doors is open, along with two opened access panels that are used for accessing the main landing-gear struts and linkages. *Ken Neubeck*

Side view of the right main landing-gear assembly shows the landing-gear door obscuring the six wheels in the main landing gear. *Ken Neubeck*

The main landing-gear assembly is referred to as two bogie assemblies, where three wheels are tied to a strut assembly. For each of the two bogie assemblies, the outside wheels are mounted together directly on a strut, whereas the interior wheel is attached by linkage to the strut. *John Gourley*

As this C-17 is taking off, each main landing-gear assembly, consisting of six wheels each, is beginning the process of tucking into the wheel well inside the lower fuselage. When the wheel assemblies are inside the fuselage, the landing-gear doors will close. *USAF photo by SSgt. Brian Ferguson*

Each of the two bogie assemblies consisting of three wheels will rotate 90 degrees and tuck into the wheel well after takeoff. *John Gourley*

Exterior view of the cockpit section in the forward fuselage of the C-17 shows the window setup for the pilot and copilot. In addition to the forward eye-level windows, there are additional windows that are located in the lower and upper sections of the forward fuselage. *John Gourley*

This interior view of the cockpit setup shows the pilot and copilot in the forward section, along with two observers in the back section behind the pilots. Notice that the left pilot uses the rail that surrounds the lower console as a footrest. The window setup for the aircraft provides adequate viewing. *USAF photo by TSgt. Shane A. Cuomo*

Captain Carl Miller is conducting a preflight check in the cockpit of a C-17 aircraft assigned to the 14th Airlift Squadron in Charleston, South Carolina, in September 2006. *USAF photo by A1C Sam Hymas*

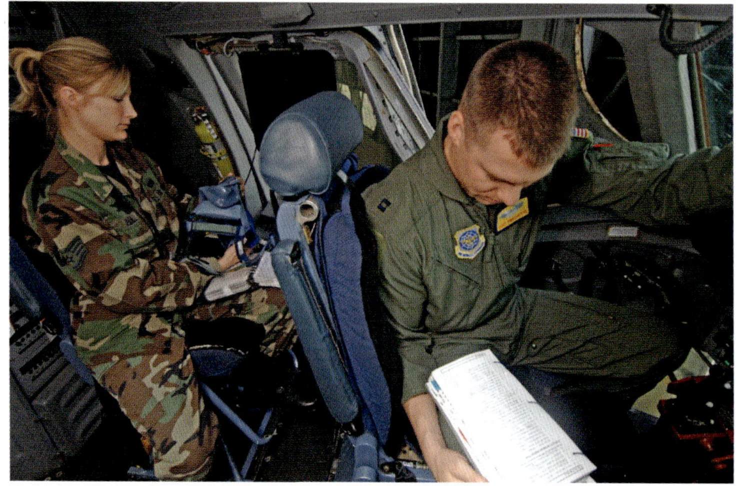

Capt. Scot Frechette is conducting a safety check in the cockpit of a C-17 aircraft while SSgt. Sarah Hall inspects a pilot's mask for defects. *USAF photo by SSgt. April Quintanilla*

This is an overview of the busy C-17 cockpit. The center console on the floor contains several controls, along with the throttle quadrant. Among the controls are communications-panel functions, nose landing-gear control, and various controls for the cargo doors on the aircraft. The pilot station is located on the left side and the copilot station is on the right side, with each pilot having a dedicated control stick. Various types of flight control and engine control panels and displays are located in the main console that faces the pilots. *Ken Neubeck*

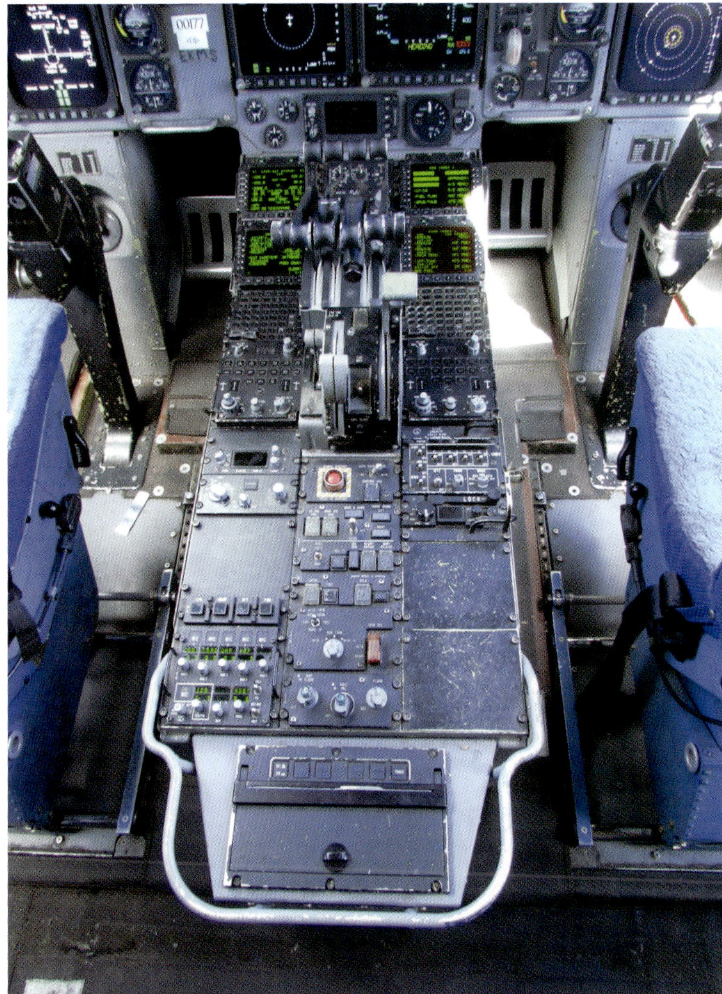

This view of the console on the floor shows the protective railing that goes around the rear portion of the console to protect it from damage when the pilots enter into their stations. Some of the control panels and associated functionality have been removed from this console for this aircraft, including the weather radar controls and the defensive control panels on the console, and at the end, the aerial-refueling slipway control handle is removed. These controls have been replaced by blank panels. Note that each pilot's seat can be adjusted forward or backward on a set of rails. *Ken Neubeck*

INSTRUMENT PANEL AND PEDESTAL

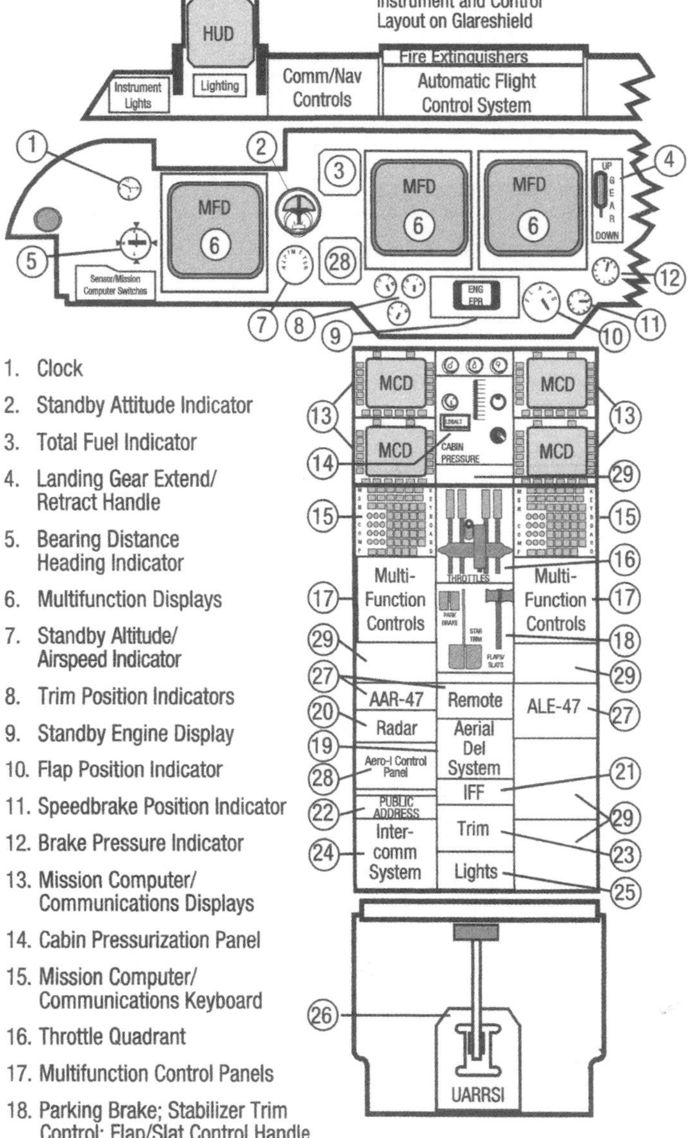

1. Clock
2. Standby Attitude Indicator
3. Total Fuel Indicator
4. Landing Gear Extend/ Retract Handle
5. Bearing Distance Heading Indicator
6. Multifunction Displays
7. Standby Altitude/ Airspeed Indicator
8. Trim Position Indicators
9. Standby Engine Display
10. Flap Position Indicator
11. Speedbrake Position Indicator
12. Brake Pressure Indicator
13. Mission Computer/ Communications Displays
14. Cabin Pressurization Panel
15. Mission Computer/ Communications Keyboard
16. Throttle Quadrant
17. Multifunction Control Panels
18. Parking Brake; Stabilizer Trim Control; Flap/Slat Control Handle
19. Aerial Delivery System Controls
20. Weather Radar Controls
21. Identification Friend/Foe (IFF) System Controls
22. Public Address Sys Controls
23. Alternate Trim Control Panel
24. Crew Intercom Controls
25. Cockpit Lighting Controls
26. Air Refuel Slipway Control Handle
27. Defensive Systems Controls
28. Aero-I Control Panel
29. Space Currently Not Used

This is a detailed diagram that shows the major control panels, displays, and indicators on the center console and in the pilot's station. The copilot's station has controls similar to those in the pilot's station. *Boeing*

Since the C-17 has gone through various upgrades during its service, some of the instruments use original monochromatic LCD displays while some of the larger LCD displays feature multicolored displays. One such monochromatic LCD display is the standby engine display / thrust rating panel (SED/TRP), which is located just above at the throttle. The author conducted reliability testing for the electronics company that built this display, beginning in 1989. *Ken Neubeck*

This close-up view near the center portion of the main console shows mechanical gauges such as the altimeter and attitude indicator, along with push-button control panels. Smaller LCD displays in the panel are a mix of monochrome black and white or green, while some of the larger LCD displays are in color. The multicolor display located in front of the control stick contains multifunction control of flaps, rudder, and aileron, along with the terrain collision avoidance system (TCAS). The left and right rudder pedals for the copilot can be seen. *Ken Neubeck*

There is a large overhead panel located in the middle of the forward cockpit that can be reached by either the pilot or copilot. This panel consists of several fuel management panels that allow for control of the fuel between the different tanks of the C-17 aircraft. *Ken Neubeck*

Located behind the overhead panel is another large circuit breaker panel assembly that consists of six rows of circuit breaker positions. It can be seen that a number of the circuit breakers have been protected or "safed" as well as being tagged, such as the APU start or drogue jettison to prevent inadvertent events from occurring during public viewing. *Ken Neubeck*

The pilot's seat has various flight controls and the control stick located in front of the pilot. Located on the left side are handles for manual openings of the windows, along with a portable light for reading maps. Note the protective rail located on the rear of the floor console. The pilot's and copilot's seats and the two observer seats are the same and contain various adjustment functions to aid in user comfort during long flights. *Ken Neubeck*

The copilot's seat has many of the same control panel functions and the same control stick as the pilot's. Manual window handles are located on the right side of the copilot. There is a heads-up display (HUD) exactly like the pilot's HUD, located on the top deck in front of the pilot, which consists of optic glass assembly with brightness and lighting control located in the assembly below the glass. *Ken Neubeck*

This wider view of the cockpit shows the busy main console area that consists of two multifunction displays in the center and an individual multifunction display for the pilot and for the copilot. Each pilot has an individual control stick and access to the engine's throttle quadrant that is located on the console between them. *Ken Neubeck*

On the ground, the crew may elect to open the side window in the cockpit through the use of a lever that is located on the bottom of the frame and allows the window to slide backward toward the rear of the aircraft. *John Gourley*

Pilots from the 7th Airlift Squadron operate a C-17 that is taking off at night from the flight line of Fort Bragg, North Carolina, during Operation Panther Storm, on July 27, 2017. The multicolor displays can be seen, along with the NVIS-compliant green lighting used on the individual control panels located inside of the main panel and overhead console. *USAF photo by SSgt. Keith James*

This is a view from the outside of the cockpit area, with an open window on the pilot side. The side window slides on rails to behind the rear window. *Ken Neubeck*

The C-17 is powered by four Pratt & Whitney F117 jet engines that are mounted in front of the wings, with two engines on each wing. The F117 engine is a military version of the same PW2000 engines that are used in the Boeing 757 commercial aircraft. *Ken Neubeck*

Engine maintenance can be performed on the F117 engines without removing the engine from the C-17 aircraft, through the use of maintenance stands that allow the maintainer to work around the engine. *USAF photo by SrA Aaron J. Jenne*

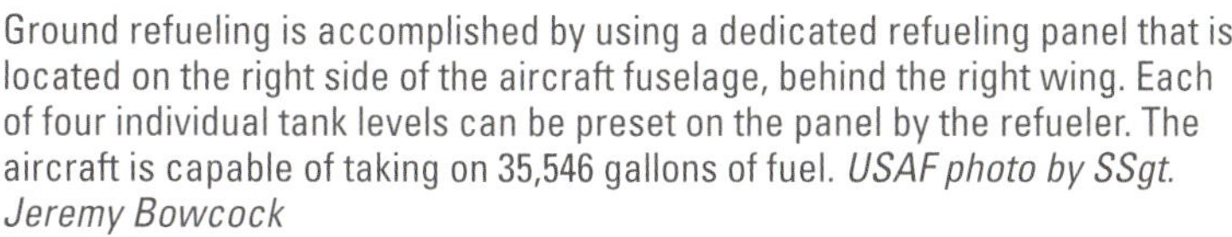

Ground refueling is accomplished by using a dedicated refueling panel that is located on the right side of the aircraft fuselage, behind the right wing. Each of four individual tank levels can be preset on the panel by the refueler. The aircraft is capable of taking on 35,546 gallons of fuel. *USAF photo by SSgt. Jeremy Bowcock*

The ground-refueling line is brought to a single-point refueling receptacle located in an access panel that is located in front of the refueling panel on the right fuselage of the aircraft. *USAF photo by SSgt. Nicole Mickle*

The C-17 has in-flight aerial-refueling capabilities through the use of a port that is located on the top of the forward fuselage, as seen here, where the C-17 is being refueled by a KC-135 Stratotanker off the coast of North Carolina in July 2016. *USAF photo by TSgt. Brandon Shapiro*

This is a view of a C-17 being refueled by a KC-135 aircraft during testing at Edwards AFB in California in July 2016. Testing also involved the KC-135, with the F-16 seen in the distance here. *USAF*

This C-17 aircraft is landing at Long Island MacArthur Airport in May 2021 to bring both maintenance crew and support equipment in order to support the USAF Thunderbirds airshow activities at Jones Beach. As indicated by the direction of the windsock in this photo, the aircraft is flying with a significant crosswind. *Ken Neubeck*

This is a subsequent view of the same C-17 aircraft during the landing sequence as it approaches the Long Island MacArthur Airport. *Ken Neubeck*

This is a C-17 aircraft from Travis AFB being refueled on the ground at Long Island MacArthur Airport in May 2021. The ground refueling port is located behind the main landing gears. The aircraft holds up to 35,500 US gallons of fuel. *Ken Neubeck*

This C-17 aircraft with the 437th Airlift Wing flies through the clouds in the southeastern US after it was refueled by a KC-135 Stratotanker. The only way to get a true bird's-eye view of a C-17 in flight is from a refueling aircraft. *US ANG photo by A1C Tiffany A. Emery*

This rear view of the left wing reveals the massive structure of the wing as well as the four flap hinge fairings that protrude in the rear of each wing. *Ken Neubeck*

A side view of the outboard engine nacelle structure is seen here, along with the extended exhaust section of the engine. *Ken Neubeck*

This rear view of the aircraft shows that each engine is mounted on an extension that is forward of the wing. *Ken Neubeck*

Side view of the wing shows the extension for each engine that allows for sufficient spacing below as well as in front of the wing. At the end of each wing is a winglet, which is 9 feet in height and has a vertical angle of 15 degrees. *Ken Neubeck*

Side view of the front of the aircraft shows the engines location and the nose landing gear. As indicated on the nose, this C-17 is assigned to both of the 60th and the 349th Airlift Wings from Travis AFB, California. Members of each wing will work side by side on these aircraft. *Ken Neubeck*

Side view of the aircraft shows how the wings slant downward at an anhedral of 3 degrees. This view shows how far in front of the wing the engines are located. The wingspan covers 170 feet and has a sweep of 25 degrees.
Ken Neubeck

This is a view of the unique T-tail design for the C-17 Globemaster III aircraft, which was developed through wind tunnel testing. The tail sits at 55 feet high, with the vertical tail section set at a sweep angle of 41 degrees, and the horizontal tail section located at the top of the tail is set at a sweep of 27 degrees. *Ken Neubeck*

This rear view of the T tail of the C-17 shows the lower section of the vertical tail section opening, used for steering control. The horizontal tail section span covers 65 feet, and it has a slant downward at an anhedral of 3 degrees. The wing anhedral of 3 degrees can also be seen in this photo. *Ken Neubeck*

As is the case with a number of Douglas aircraft designs, the horizontal tail stabilizer is located high on the vertical stabilizer section of the tail. *Ken Neubeck*

The forward section of the horizontal tail stabilizer is the trimmable stabilizer, which has the ability to pivot up and down. *Ken Neubeck*

There are several flight control surfaces that are located on each wing of the C-17 aircraft. Located on the leading edge of each wing are four slats. Located on the trailing edge of each wing are two inboard flaps and one outboard aileron. There are four spoilers located just in front of the flaps. *Ken Neubeck*

During the takeoff sequence, as the pilot lifts the nosewheel, the aircraft rides on the main landing gears while the rear wing flaps are extended. *Ken Neubeck*

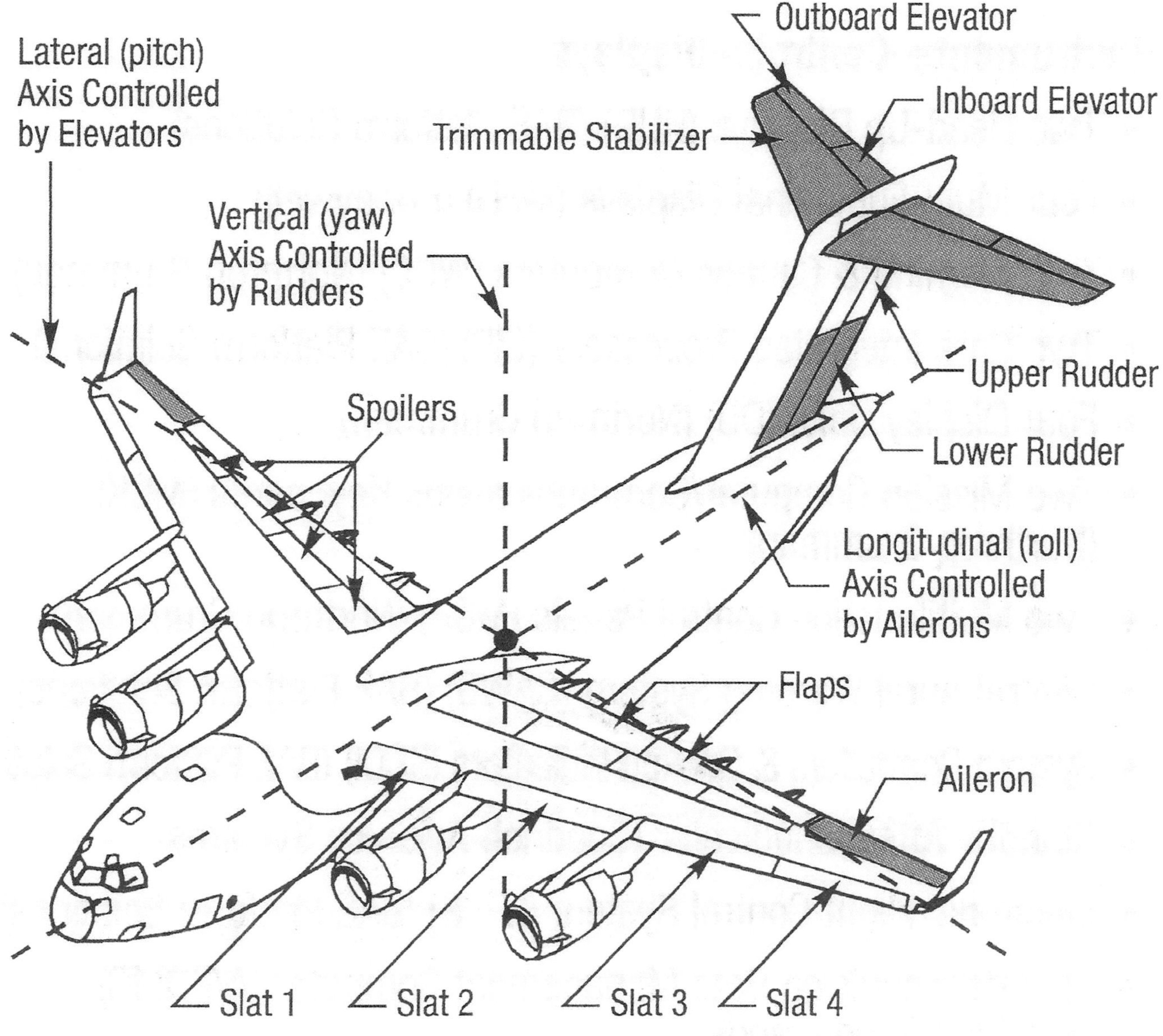

This diagram shows the location on the aircraft structure of all flight control surfaces on the C-17 aircraft. *Boeing*

C-17 takes off from Incirlik Air Base in Turkey in March 2016 with the wing flaps extended. *USAF photo by Senior Airman John Nieves Camacho*

This forward view of a C-17 aircraft as it is landing at MacArthur Airport in Long Island, New York, in May 2021, shows the rear wing flaps behind both wings being fully extended. *Ken Neubeck*

Front view of the C-17 aircraft shows that the design and geometry of the aircraft's wings take into account the clearances that are required between the engines and the ground.
Ken Neubeck

Diagram shows the critical design clearances that are required between the engines and wings to the ground, particularly when landing and taking off from unimproved airfields.

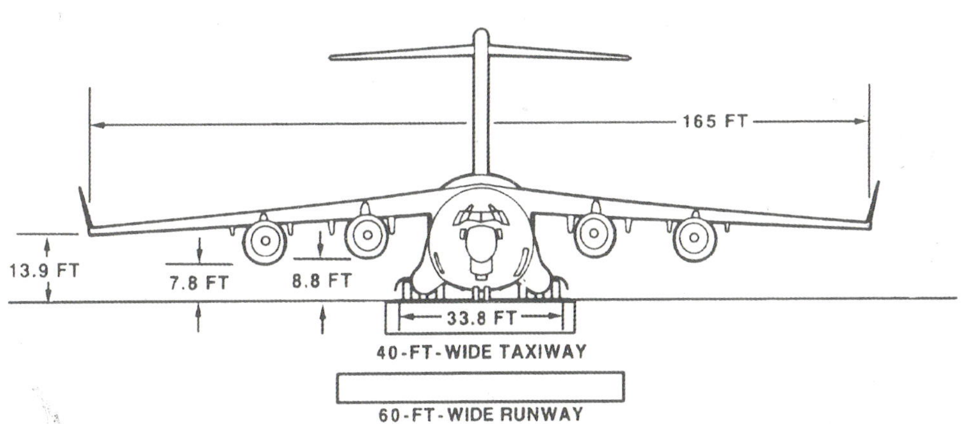

This is an outside view of the rear ramp section of the C-17 as it extends from the aircraft. There is a linkage assembly located on each side of the ramp that aids in the extension of the ramp.
Ken Neubeck

This is another view of the rear ramp section of the C-17 as it extends from the aircraft.
Ken Neubeck

This view is of the area at the rear of the C-17 where loading takes place into the rear of the cargo area. *Ken Neubeck*

The cargo hold area can be sufficiently lighted to allow nighttime loading of cargo into the C-17 rear area, as seen here during loading at Andrews AFB, Maryland. *USAF photo by TSgt. Joshua DeMotts*

The top photo shows the loading ramp lowered to the ground for cargo loaded on carts to be brought into the aircraft, whereas in the bottom photo, the loading ramp is raised to a level position in order to receive cargo from a forklift as shown. *Ken Neubeck*

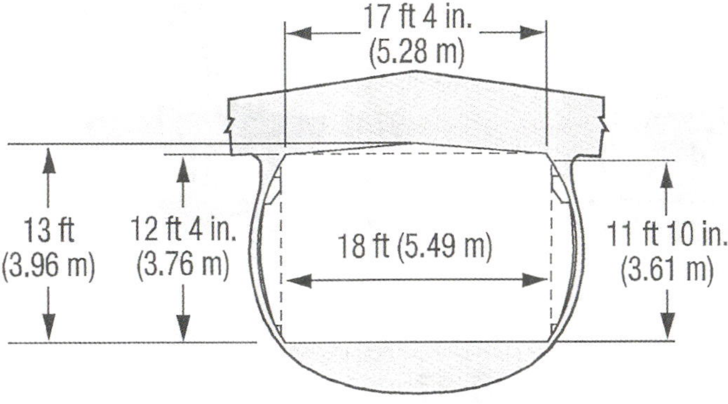

The cargo hold area of the C-17 maintains a consistent width throughout the length of the cargo area at 18 feet, as shown in the diagrams to the right. The height will vary throughout the cargo area, as shown here. *Boeing*

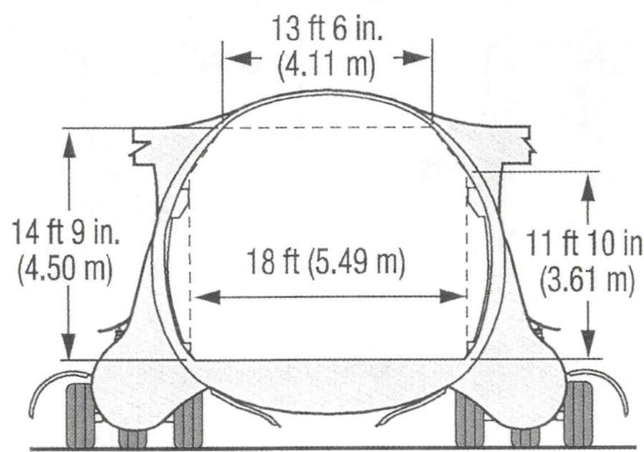

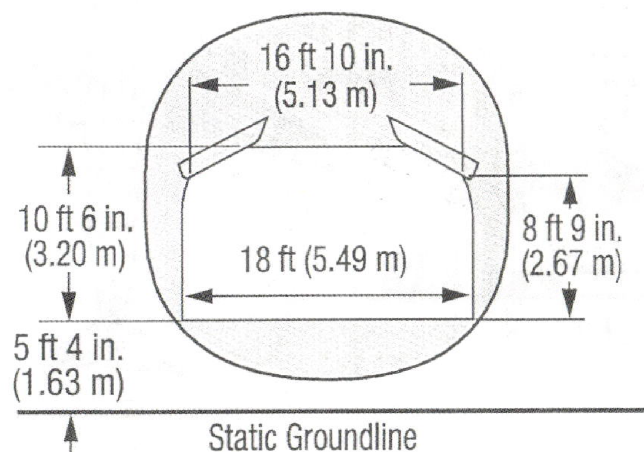

This view of the rear of the C-17 shows the cargo area. *Ken Neubeck*

View from the rear shows the two-piece ramp area of the C-17 that allows loading of equipment into the aircraft. *John Gourley*

The C-17 aircraft features track-style flooring that has numerous attachment points for attaching hardware. Various hardware items are stored along inserts in the wall. The ceiling contains lighting and cable runs for providing electric throughout the aircraft. *Ken Neubeck*

The left side of the cargo hold area of the C-17 contains cutouts for storing various attaching hardware items and restraining straps, as well as hydraulic power control panels. In addition, there is an emergency exit door for the crew. *Ken Neubeck*

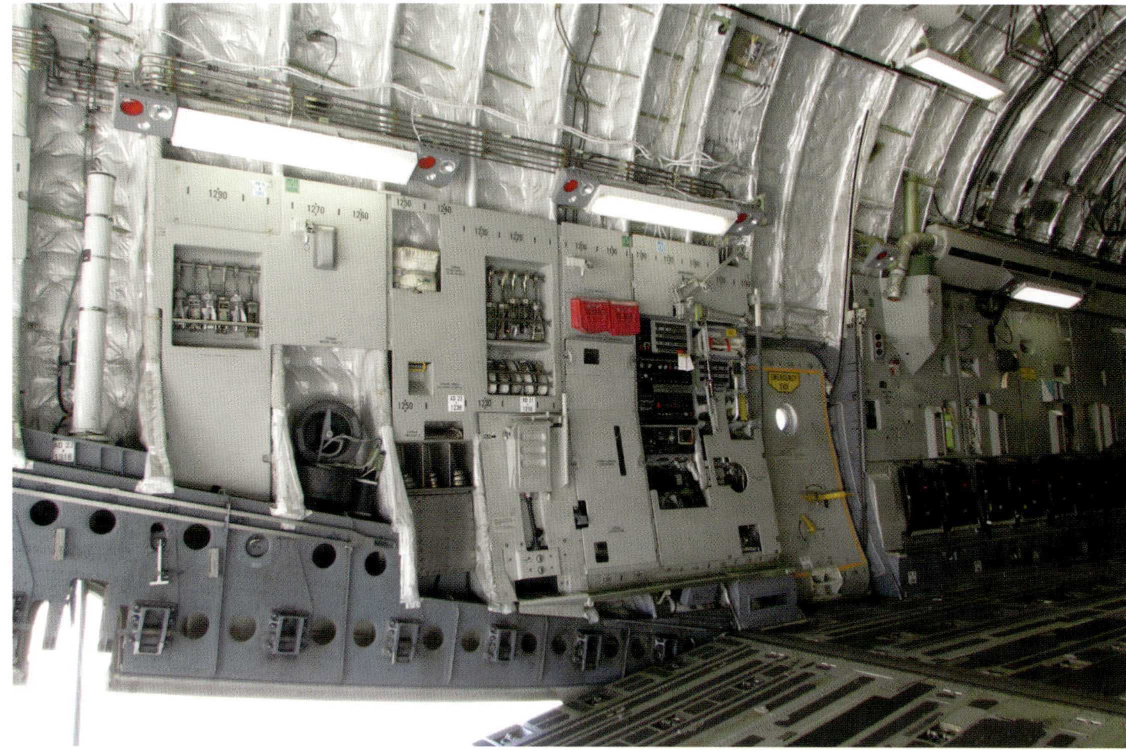

The right side of the cargo hold area of the C-17 also contains cutouts for storing various attaching hardware items, as well as control panels for electric power. There is an emergency exit door on this side as well. *Ken Neubeck*

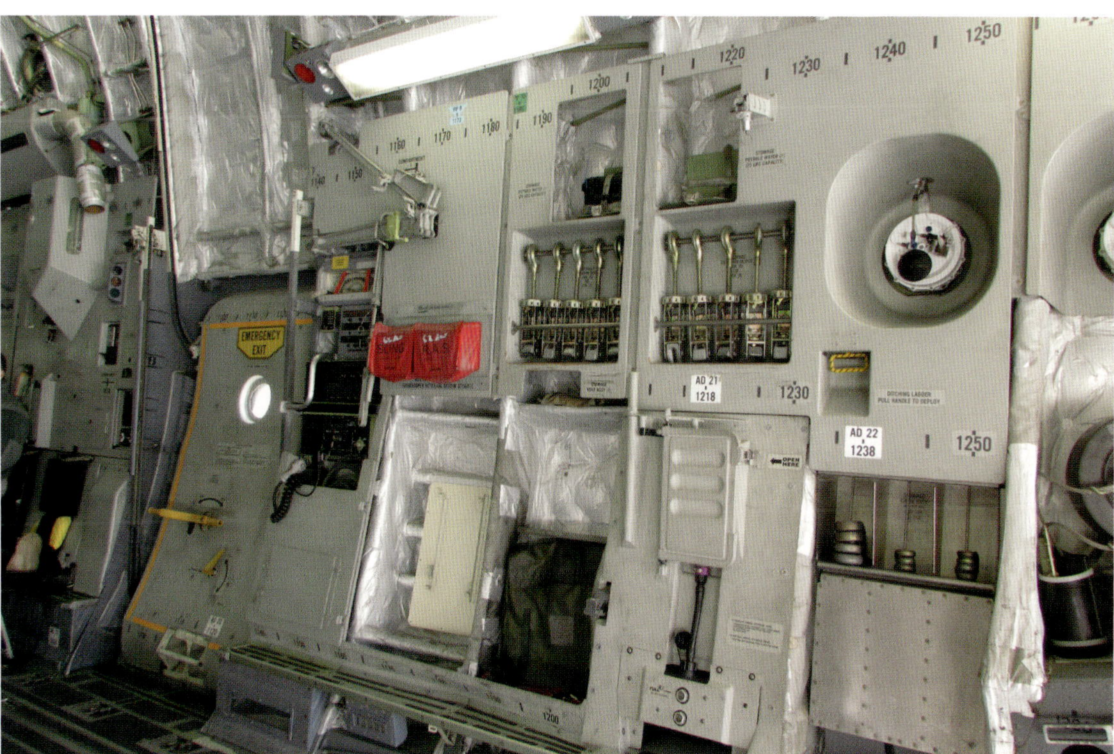

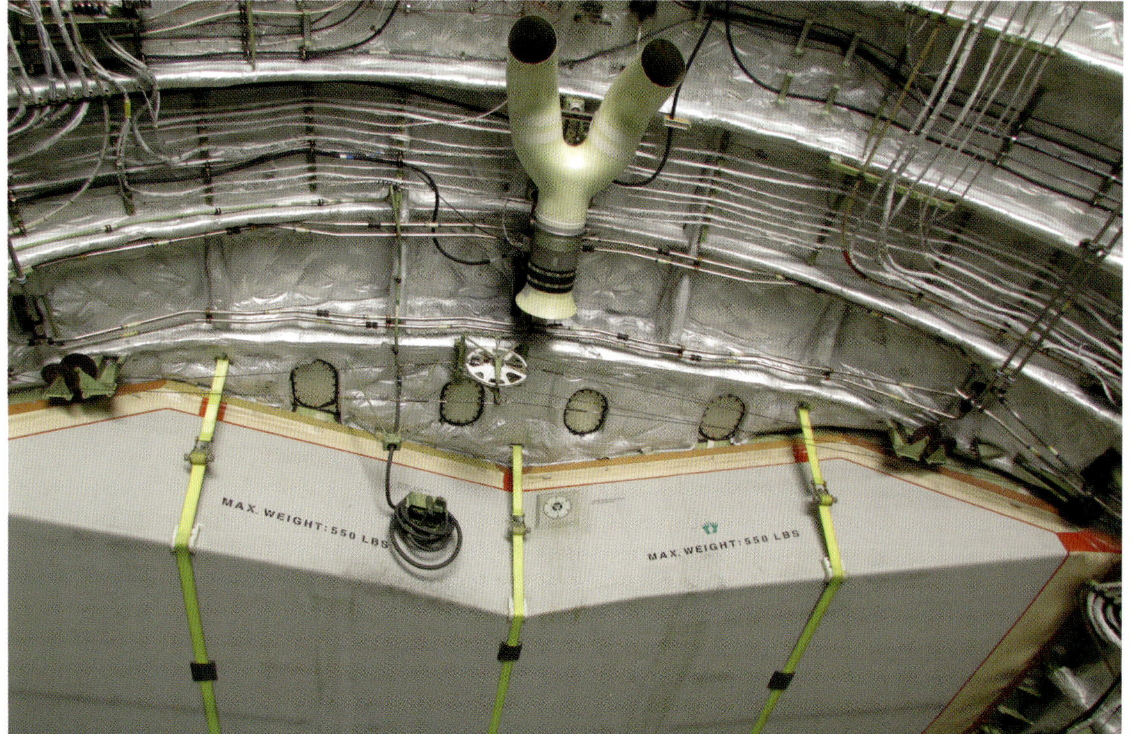

The ceiling area near the center of the C-17 cargo area contains some ducting attached to the ceiling, along with electrical wiring. Additionally, the wing box of the aircraft is visible, along with some restraining straps for cargo. *Ken Neubeck*

Toward the front of the cargo area is the rear of the cockpit area. Access to the cockpit is via a set of stairs located below the cockpit (seen here below the American flag). There are two emergency doors located at cockpit level (on either side of the flag). Ductwork and electrical wiring can be seen along the ceiling area as well. *Ken Neubeck*

There is a viewing window located in between the front cockpit doors. Electronic boxes and cables are located toward the ceiling between the two doors as well. *Ken Neubeck*

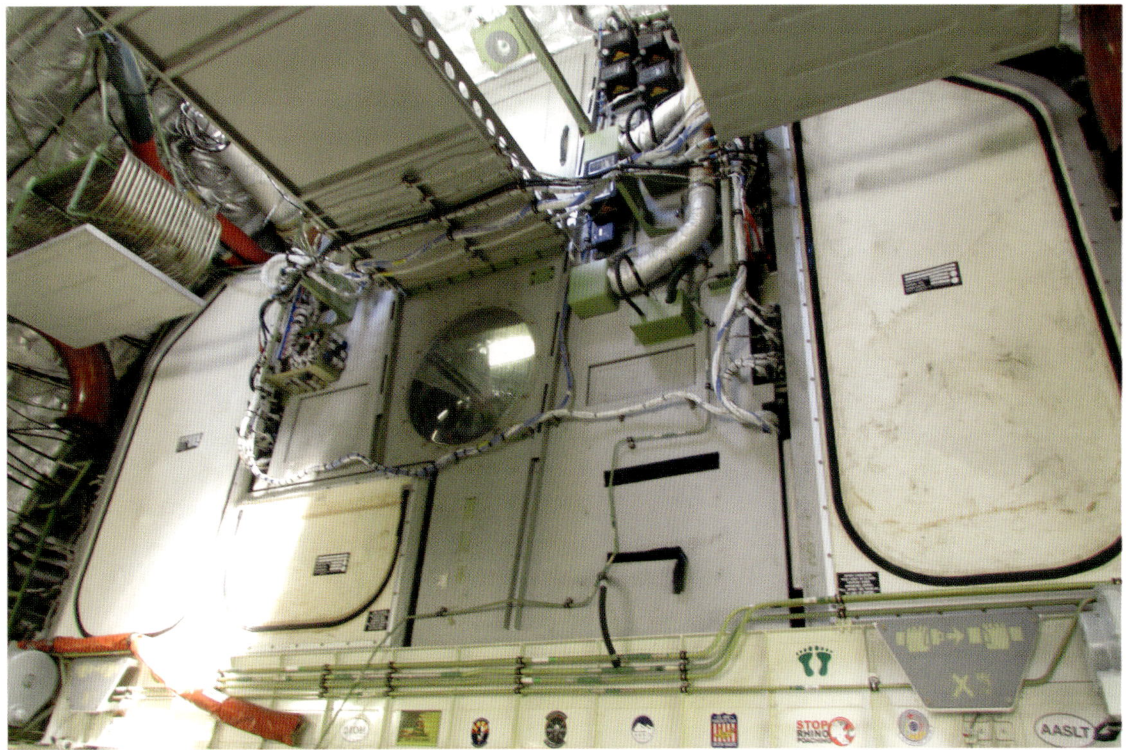

Located on the left sidewall of the front of the cargo area are numerous electrical-wiring and heating vents. In addition, there is a heat exchanger unit located on a shelf that is above the left cockpit door. *Ken Neubeck*

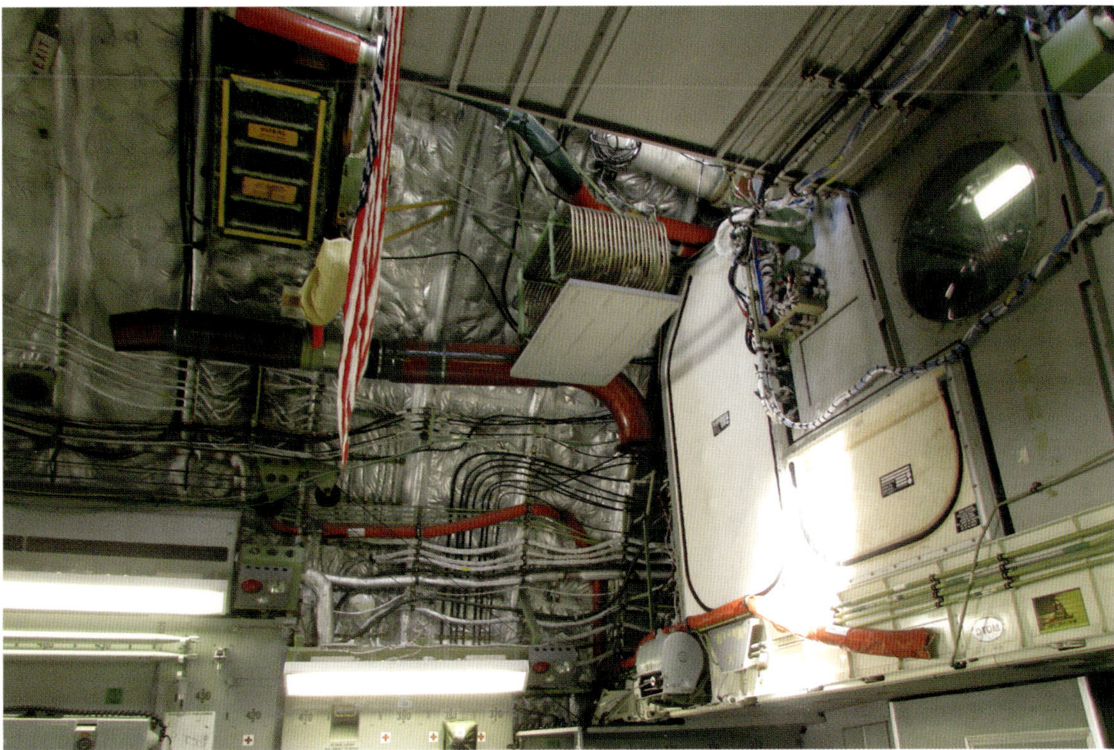

Lined up on each wall of the cargo area are troop seats that fold up into the wall and are extended when needed. *John Gourley*

Located on the left inside wall toward the front of the cargo area are an emergency medical kit, emergency oxygen with mask, electrical power outlets, and landing-gear down-lock pins. *Ken Neubeck*

This view toward the rear of the cargo area shows the unique uneven floor design, with slots and holes used to accommodate tie-down restraints as well as seat attachment points. *Ken Neubeck*

Rear view of the loading entrance of the C-17 shows the loading ramp and the area surrounding the ramp. *Ken Neubeck*

CHAPTER 4

Loadmaster Functions

The C-17 crew of three consists of the pilot and copilot, along with probably the most important member with regard to the mission of the aircraft: the loadmaster. It is the loadmaster who has to develop the planning scheme for the proper loading of the aircraft with equipment and people for the specified mission that the aircraft is to fly. The aircraft has to have even and balanced weight distribution in the cargo area in order for it to be able to take off and land properly, as well as being able to fly straight and level with the loads inside.

The loadmaster plans for the proper equipment needed to secure the cargo, such as chains and tie-downs. With regard to personnel, the loadmaster is responsible for the passenger-seating configuration in the cargo hold area.

There are a number of missions that the C-17 flies, each of which requires the precise attention of the loadmaster. The following pages show the loadmaster in action, along with the different scenarios for the C-17 as described in the C-17 operations manual.

At the end of this section, there are photos and descriptions of some of the maintenance tasks that are performed on the C-17 by ground crew.

This C-17 loadmaster is near the rear of the aircraft, using the hydraulic control panel to actuate the air delivery system (ADS) for closing the rear door. *USAF photo by TSgt. Dennis J. Henry*

A C-17 loadmaster is filling hydraulic fluid in the hydraulic service reservoir during repair action on C-17 during Hurricane Sandy relief in the northeastern United States in November 2012. *USAF photo by SSgt. Sean Tobin*

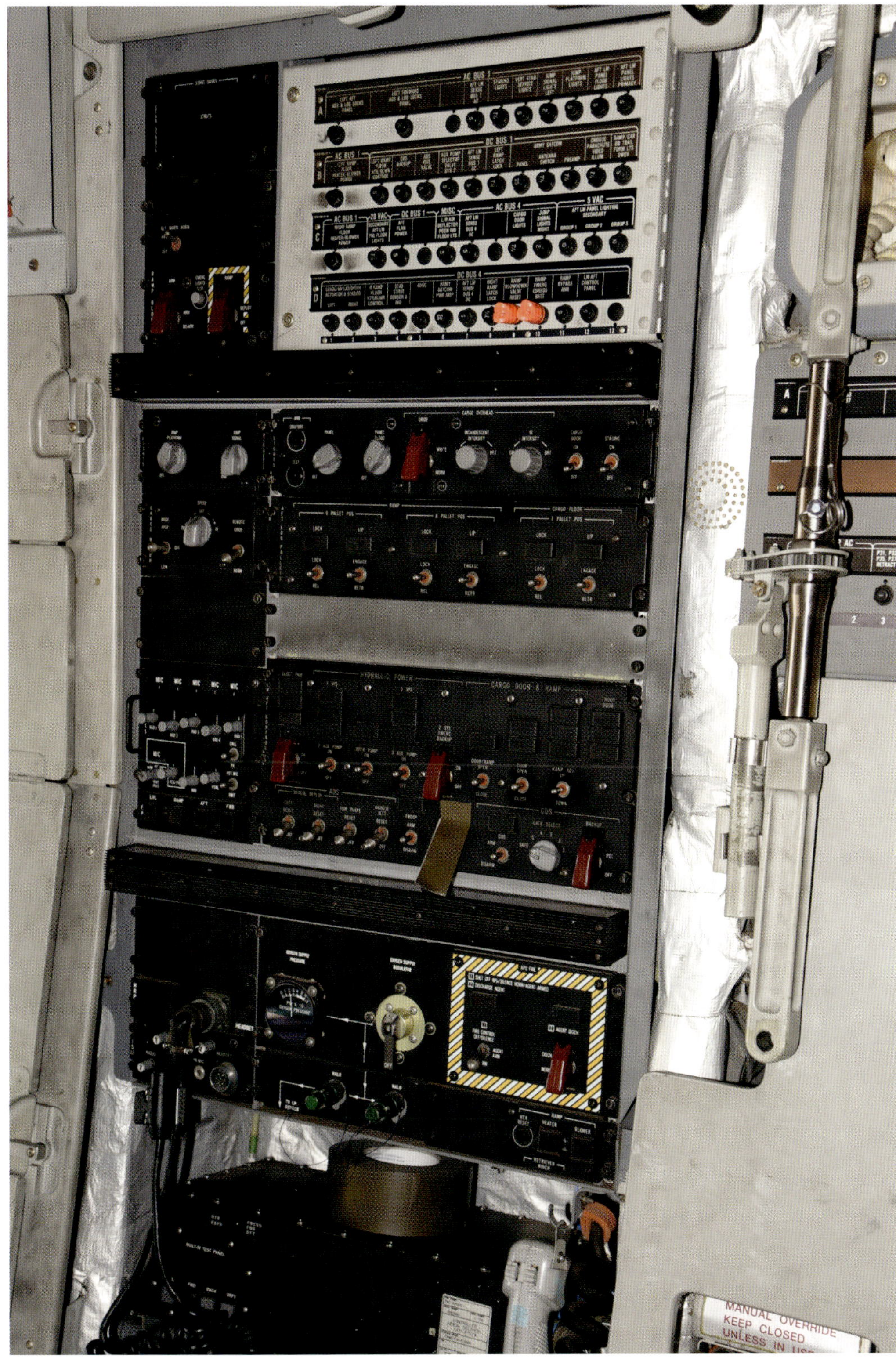

An important set of controls for the loadmaster are located on the right side of the cargo area, near the rear. The top panel is a circuit breaker panel for various electrical functions in the cargo area, and below that is the lighting-control panel. Below that panel is the pallet control panel, and below that is the hydraulic power control panel. The gauge on the lowest panel is the oxygen supply gauge, with the regulator switch to the right of it. The special marked rectangle on that panel is the APU fire extinguisher control panel. *John Gourley*

This C-17 loadmaster is at his station near the steps to the cockpit area of the aircraft. A number of control panels are located in this area. Located in the panel to the left is the Onboard Inert Generating Gas System (OBIGGS) control panel. *USAF photo by SrA Jennifer L. Flores*

Close-up view of the panels that are part of the loadmaster's station. The panel shown on the left shows the OBIGGS control panel located on the bottom, whereas the set of control panels in the station on the right shows various controls for cargo hold lighting, ramp and door controls, drogue control, and a series of circuit breakers for these controls. *John Gourley*

Defense Transportation Regulation – Part III Mobility

15 October 2019

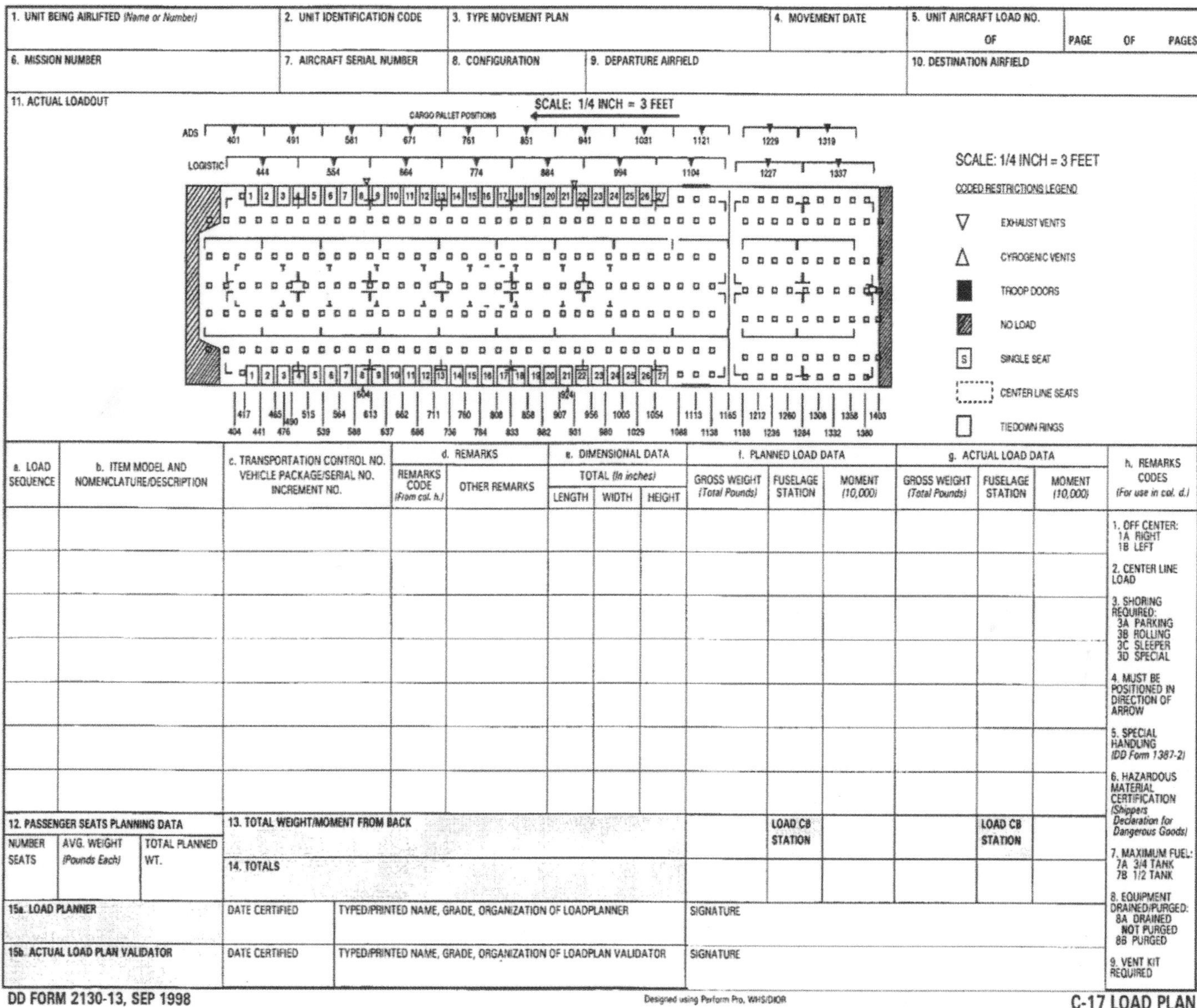

1. UNIT BEING AIRLIFTED *(Name or Number)*	2. UNIT IDENTIFICATION CODE	3. TYPE MOVEMENT PLAN	4. MOVEMENT DATE	5. UNIT AIRCRAFT LOAD NO. OF	PAGE OF PAGES
6. MISSION NUMBER	7. AIRCRAFT SERIAL NUMBER	8. CONFIGURATION	9. DEPARTURE AIRFIELD	10. DESTINATION AIRFIELD	

11. ACTUAL LOADOUT

a. LOAD SEQUENCE	b. ITEM MODEL AND NOMENCLATURE/DESCRIPTION	c. TRANSPORTATION CONTROL NO. VEHICLE PACKAGE/SERIAL NO. INCREMENT NO.	d. REMARKS: REMARKS CODE *(From col. h.)*	d. REMARKS: OTHER REMARKS	e. DIMENSIONAL DATA TOTAL *(In inches)*: LENGTH	WIDTH	HEIGHT	f. PLANNED LOAD DATA: GROSS WEIGHT *(Total Pounds)*	FUSELAGE STATION	MOMENT *(10,000)*	g. ACTUAL LOAD DATA: GROSS WEIGHT *(Total Pounds)*	FUSELAGE STATION	MOMENT *(10,000)*	h. REMARKS CODES *(For use in col. d.)*
														1. OFF CENTER: 1A RIGHT 1B LEFT
														2. CENTER LINE LOAD
														3. SHORING REQUIRED: 3A PARKING 3B ROLLING 3C SLEEPER 3D SPECIAL
														4. MUST BE POSITIONED IN DIRECTION OF ARROW
														5. SPECIAL HANDLING *(DD Form 1387-2)*
														6. HAZARDOUS MATERIAL CERTIFICATION *(Shippers Declaration for Dangerous Goods)*

12. PASSENGER SEATS PLANNING DATA			13. TOTAL WEIGHT/MOMENT FROM BACK		LOAD CB STATION			LOAD CB STATION		7. MAXIMUM FUEL: 7A 3/4 TANK 7B 1/2 TANK
NUMBER SEATS	AVG. WEIGHT *(Pounds Each)*	TOTAL PLANNED WT.	14. TOTALS							
15a. LOAD PLANNER			DATE CERTIFIED	TYPED/PRINTED NAME, GRADE, ORGANIZATION OF LOADPLANNER	SIGNATURE					8. EQUIPMENT DRAINED/PURGED: 8A DRAINED NOT PURGED 8B PURGED
15b. ACTUAL LOAD PLAN VALIDATOR			DATE CERTIFIED	TYPED/PRINTED NAME, GRADE, ORGANIZATION OF LOADPLAN VALIDATOR	SIGNATURE					9. VENT KIT REQUIRED

DD FORM 2130-13, SEP 1998 — Designed using Perform Pro, WHS/DIOR — C-17 LOAD PLAN

For each C-17 mission, the loadmaster uses this government form to plan out the loading requirements for the aircraft, which includes both the sequence and the location of the loads involved.

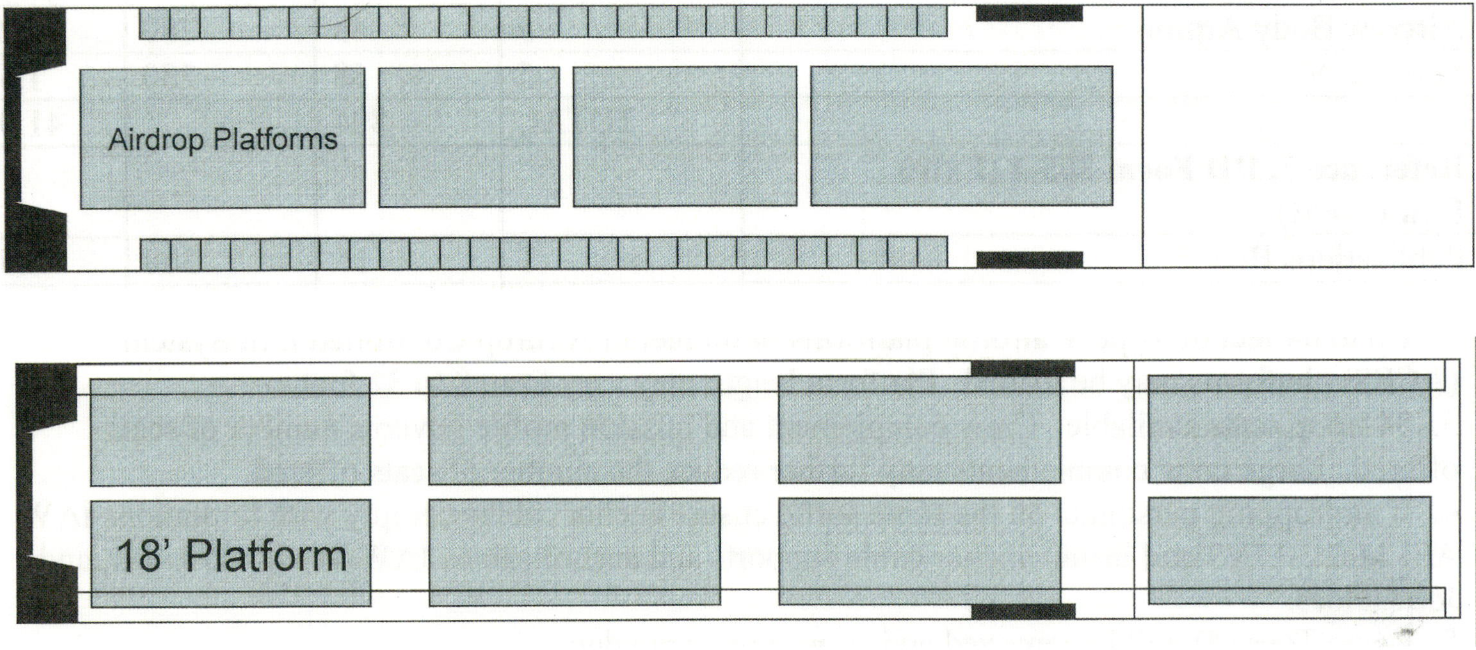

Above are two configurations for dropping pallets through the rear doors of the C-17 while in flight.

A cargo pallet with parachute is being dropped out of the rear cargo doors of a C-17 during an airdrop exercise during Rainier War at Moses Lake, Washington, in December 2015. The cargo area is set up in ADC-2 configuration for the airdrop, as shown in the figure above. *USAF photo by SrA Divine Cox*

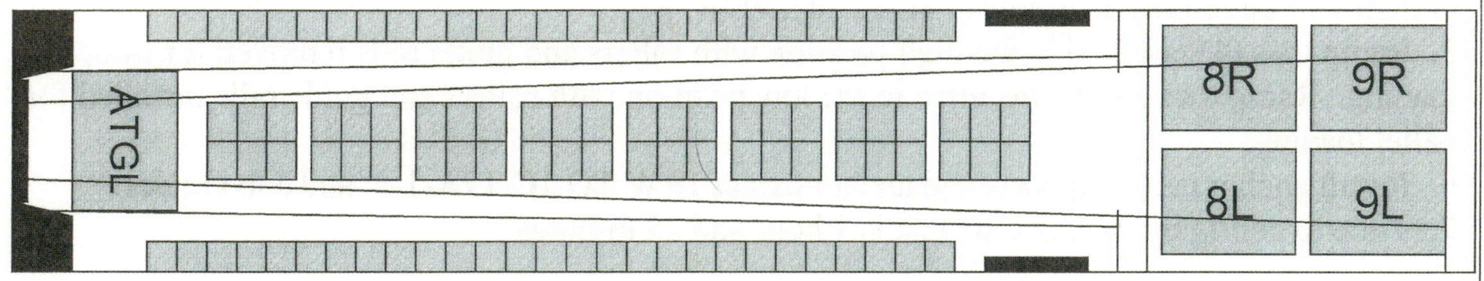

Above is the ADP-1 configuration that is used for dropping paratroopers through the rear door of the C-17 while in flight.

On July 12, 2016, 82nd Airborne Division troops prepare to jump on Sicily Drop Zone out of a C-17 Globemaster III during battalion mass tactical-training week at Pope Army Airfield, North Carolina. This configuration allows for 102 troop seats for the airborne paratroopers, as shown in the figure above. *USAF photo by SSgt. Sandra Welch*

C-1 configuration

There are three different cargo configurations used in the cargo area of the C-17: C1, C2, and C3. This photo shows the C-1 configuration. Fifty-nine Los Angeles firemen occupy the troop seats on the sides and one section in the middle, while eight pallets of relief aid occupy the middle of the cargo area. *USAF photo by Airman 1st Class Taylor Queen*

C-2 configuration

This is a version of the C-2 configuration in which troops from the 143rd Infantry Regiment are seated in the troop seats on the sides while two US Army vehicles occupy the center of the cargo area, during training exercises held at Altus AFB in March 2015. *USAF photo by SrA J. Zuriel Lee*

Pallets containing over 83,000 pounds of rice are secured in the cargo area of a C-17 from the 62nd Airlift Wing. The rice was delivered to Honduras during a humanitarian mission to provide food for orphanages, schools, and feeding programs for children. This configuration is the C-3 configuration, in which the center of the cargo area is loaded with pallets, and the troop seats located on the sides are in the stowed position. *USAF photo by SrA Tryphena Mayhugh*

1R	2R	3R	4R	5R	6R	7R	8R	9R
1L	2L	3L	4L	5L	6L	7L	8L	9L

C-3 configuration

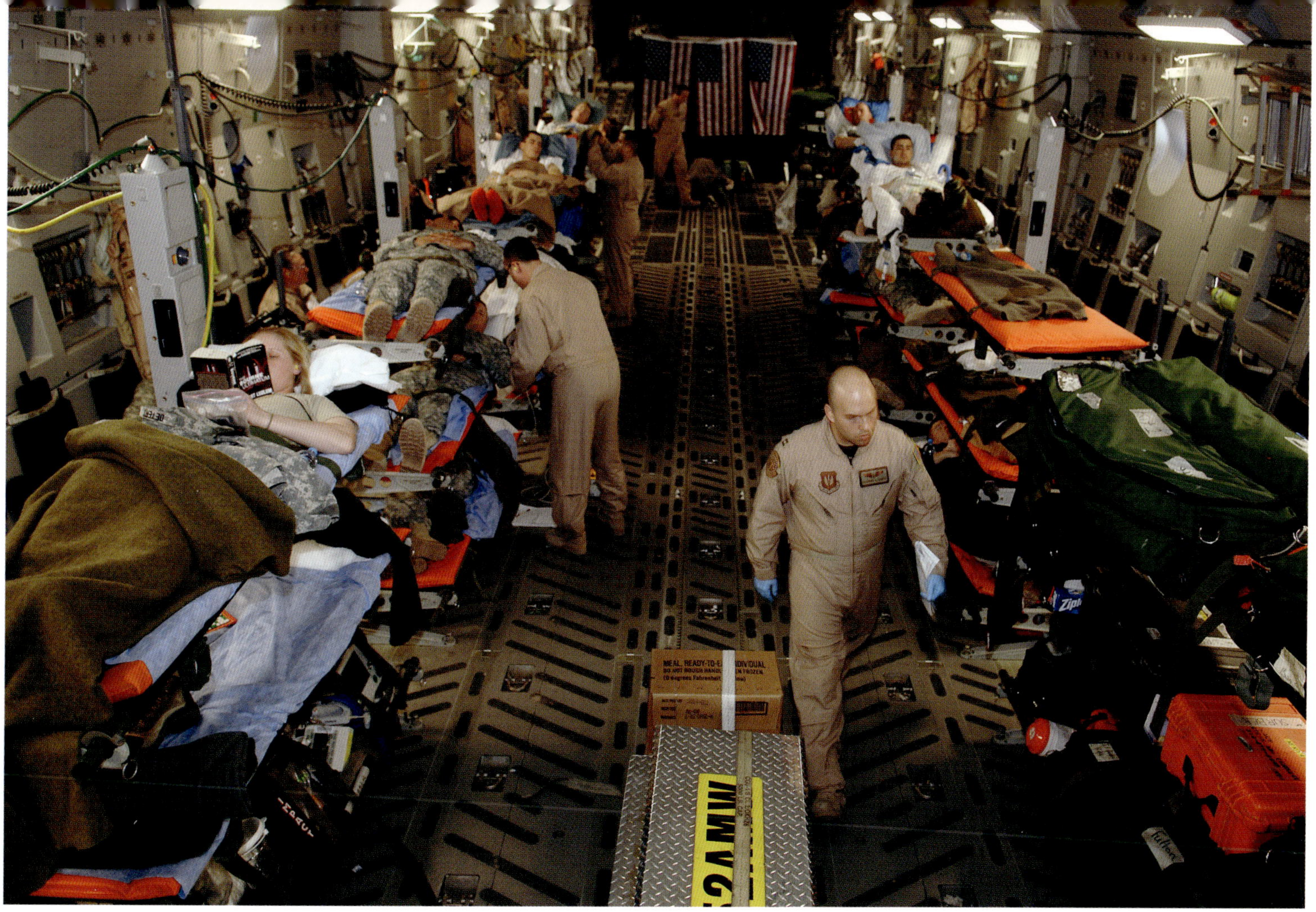

Members of the 791st Expeditionary Aeromedical Evacuation Squadron monitor patients during an aeromedical evacuation mission from Balad Air Base, Iraq, to Ramstein Air Base, Germany, on February 25, 2007. The AE-2 configuration is used. *USAF photo by MSgt. Scott Reed*

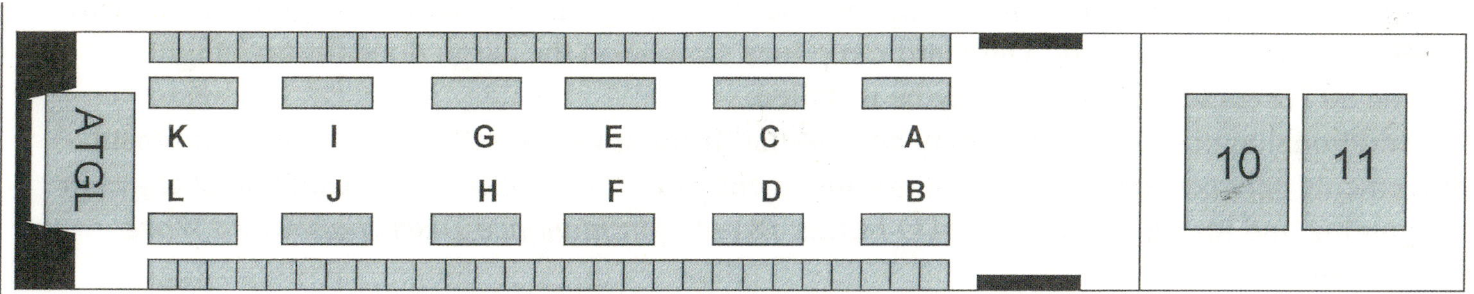

There are three different configurations for aeromedical evacuation: AE-1, AE-2, and AE-3. The diagram above is an example of AE-2 configuration in which medical stations are set up along the walls of the cargo area.

US Army troops from the 1st Battalion, 503rd Infantry Regiment, 173rd Airborne Brigade, are riding with the Italian army's 186th Airborne Regiment, Forlgore Brigade, during the Bayonet Strike exercise in June 2018 at Aviano Air Base, Italy. Troops are using the pullout seats from the sides of the cargo area, along with a center row installed into the cargo floor. This configuration allows for 102 seats. *ANG photo by SrA John Linzmeier*

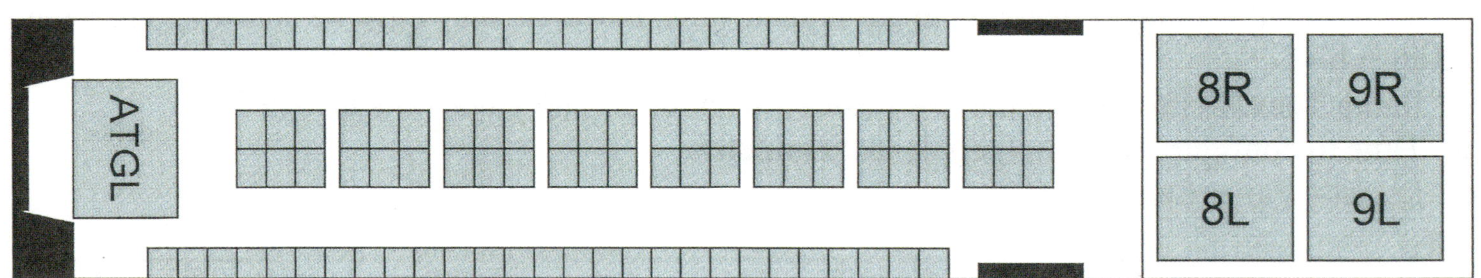

Above is the P-1, or passenger transfer, configuration.

C-17 aircraft is on display at Stewart AFB during the 2015 New York State Air Show, with the cargo area opened. A US Army truck is located in the rear of the cargo area as part of the SD-1 configuration. *Ken Neubeck*

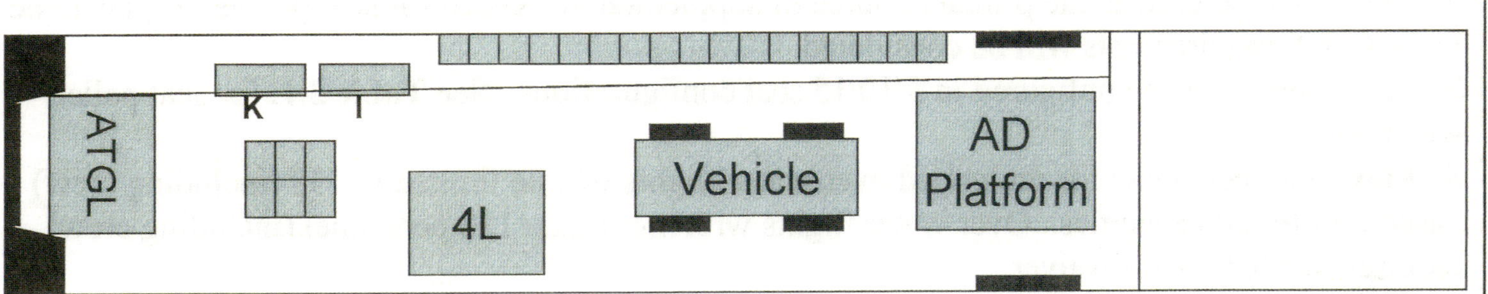

Above is the SD-1 configuration of the cargo area when the C-17 is set up for static display during events at air force bases and air shows.

USAF personnel are setting up chains to attachment points on the floor in preparation to tying down pallets of supplies. *USAF photo by MSgt. Andy Dunaway*

A USAF crew member is setting up the proper tension on the chains securing two Humvee vehicles to the floor in the cargo hold area. *USAF photo by MSgt. Benjamin S. Bloker*

USAF personnel are setting up chains to secure a PZH-2000 howitzer from the Netherlands for transport from Ramstein Air Base, Germany, to Afghanistan in 2006. *USAF photo by MSgt. John E. Lasky*

USAF personnel are using a winch system to pull a HH-60 Pave Hawk into the cargo area of a C-17 while deployed to Iraq in 2008. *USAF photo by SrA Juliane Showalter*

A cargo loader waits as airmen move equipment in place on a C-17 aircraft in March 14, 2014, at the transit center at Manas, Kyrgyzstan. The cargo is being loaded in preparation for base closure in July 2014. *USAF photo by SrA Ross Alexander Whitley*

Airmen from the 535th Airlift Squadron push a pallet into the cargo area of a C-17 in October 2016, in preparation for a training exercise in the Pohakuloa training area in Hawaii. *US Army photo by SSgt. Armondo R. Limon*

A1C Alexia Lewis is a loadmaster for the 21st Airlift Squadron and is in the process of having a Tunner loader being placed into the cargo area of the aircraft. She is part of an all-female crew to mark Women's History Month via this flight on March 18, 2018, at Anderson AFB, Guam. *USAF photo by Heide Couch*

An aircraft tug, which is used to move extremely heavy aircraft, now assigned to the 911th Airlift Wing, sits in the cargo area ready for takeoff at Dobbins Air Reserve Base, Georgia, on April 11, 2019. The aircraft tug is counterweighted by approximately 40,000 pounds of weights to balance the C-17 aircraft, as established by the loadmaster. *USAF photo by SrA Grace Thomson*

A 212th Rescue Squadron pararescueman performs a military free fall from the rear of a C-17 aircraft from the 249th Airlift Squadron in October 2015, near the coast of White Beach Naval Base, Japan. *USAF*

Cargo for the 82nd Airborne Division is air-dropped through the rear of the cargo area of a C-17 over North Carolina in October 2015, during a joint training operation. *USAF photo by SrA Divine Cox*

This view from the front of the cargo area of the C-17, looking toward the rear of the aircraft, shows that the floor is uneven. The unique floor setup has indentations in different sections that is configured to handle different types of cargo. *Ken Neubeck*

Bird's-eye view of the cargo hold floor shows the different slots and holes that are located throughout each section of the floor. Here, airmen from the 945th Aircraft Maintenance Squadron go over their inspection notes for a C-17 aircraft prior to takeoff from Travis AFB, California. *USAF photo by SSgt. Daniel Phelps*

This C-17 is undergoing a 720-day home station refurb inspection at Altus AFB, Oklahoma, where many of the panels of the aircraft are opened for inspection by maintenance personnel. *USAF photo by SrA Jesse Lopez*

Maintenance personnel are using a lift to replace a forward slot section on the right wing, in addition to performing engine maintenance. *USAF photo by Sue Sapp*

Maintenance personnel are performing engine maintenance while using a maintenance stand to open access panels to reach the engine. *USAF*

Maintenance personnel is performing checks with tools on the C-17 main landing-gear assembly. *USAF photo by TSgt. James Hodgman*

An aircraft maintenance trainer that consists of the front portion of the C-17 aircraft for training C-17 maintenance personnel is available at the 373rd Training Detachment Squadron, located at Travis AFB, California. *USAF photo by SSgt. Patrick Hallower*

Maintenance personnel are training on performing engine maintenance while using the aircraft engine maintenance trainer that is located at the 373rd Training Detachment Squadron, located at Travis AFB. *USAF photo by SSgt Patrick Hallower*

CHAPTER 5

USAF Squadrons

The C-17 is operated by two groups in the United States: the US Air Force and the US Air National Guard (ANG). Some locations, such as Elmendorf Air Force Base (AFB) in Alaska and Hickam AFB in Hawaii, support both the USAF and ANG airlift wings that are at those locations.

The first C-17 wing was the 437th Airlift Wing at Charleston AFB, South Carolina, with the wing receiving its first C-17 in 1993. The most recent base to receive its first C-17 is the ANG at Charlotte, North Carolina, in 2018.

The various airlift wings support many different missions, both military and nonmilitary, around the world. The Globemaster III squadrons are as follows:

Active US Air Force C-17 Wings and Squadrons

Airlift Mobility Wing	Airlift Squadron	Location	Year to C-17 aircraft
3rd	517th	Elmendorf AFB, AK	2007
15th	535th	Hickam AFB, HI	2005
60th	21st	Travis AFB, CA	2006
62nd	4th, 7th, 8th	McChord AFB, WA	1999
97th	58th	Altus AFB, OK	1996
305th	6th	McGuire-Lakehurst AFB, NJ	2004
349th (Reserve)	301st	Travis AFB, CA	2006
436th	3rd	Dover AFB, DE	2007
437th	14th, 15th, 16th	Charleston AFB, SC	1993

Active Air National Guard C-17 Squadrons

Airlift Mobility Wing	Airlift Squadron	Location	Year to C-17 aircraft
105th	137th	Stewart AFB, NY	2011
145th	156th	Charlotte ANGB, NC	2018
154th	204th	Hickam AFB, HI	2006
164th	155th	Memphis ANGB, TN	2012
167th	167th	Martinsburg ANG, WV	2015
172nd	183rd	Jackson ANGB, MS	2004
176th	144th	Elmendorf AFB, AK	2017

Active USAF C-17 Units

The 3rd Wing at Elmendorf AFB, Alaska, was activated in June 2007. Here is one of the first C-17 aircraft delivered to this wing, as it flies over the Alaska mountain range. *USAF photo by TSgt. Keith Brown*

Close-up view of this 3rd Airlift Wing C-17 shows that the aircraft is assigned to the 517th Airlift Squadron and the aircraft is named the "Spirit of Denali." The name refers to the highest mountain point in the United States. *USAF photo by TSgt. Keith Brown*

This C-17 aircraft from the 535th Airlift Squadron of 15th Airlift Wing, out of Hickam AFB, is flying over Waianae Range, Hawaii, in October 2016. *USAF photo by SSgt. Armando Limon*

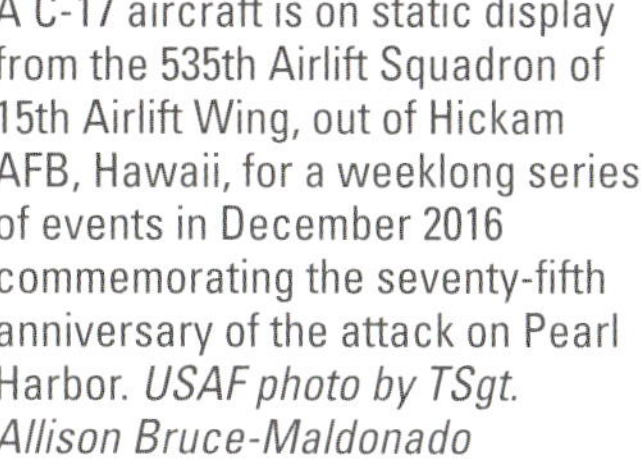

A C-17 aircraft is on static display from the 535th Airlift Squadron of 15th Airlift Wing, out of Hickam AFB, Hawaii, for a weeklong series of events in December 2016 commemorating the seventy-fifth anniversary of the attack on Pearl Harbor. *USAF photo by TSgt. Allison Bruce-Maldonado*

The 60th Airlift Wing at Travis AFB, California, receives its first C-17 aircraft during a ceremony in August 2006. This C-17 was nicknamed the Spirit of Solano. *USAF photo by SSgt. Mat McGovern*

C-17 "Spirit of Solano" (tail number 06-6154) is seen here in May 2021 at MacArthur Airport in Long Island, New York, in support of the USAF Thunderbirds airs how at Jones Beach. A special "Spirit of Solano" emblem is located under the US Air Force marking on the main forward fuselage. *Ken Neubeck*

This C-17 aircraft from the 62nd Airlift Wing is dispensing countermeasure flares over Selah Air Base in Yakima, Washington, in November 2018. *USAF photo by SrA Tryphena Mayhugh*

A C-17 aircraft from the 62nd Airlift Wing is landing on the newly resurfaced runway at McChord Field in Washington in June 2019. The 4th, 5th, 6th, and 7th Airlift Squadrons operate at this base. *USAF photo by A1C Sara Hoerich*

Eleven C-17 aircraft line up on the Moses Lake runway in December 2015, during airdrop exercise during Rainier War at Moses Lake, Washington. Rainier War is a semiannual large-formation exercise that is hosted by the 62nd Airlift Wing, designed to train aircrews under realistic scenarios. *USAF photo by SrA Divine Cox*

C-17 aircraft from the 62nd Airlift Wing has just completed a parachute drop in May 2021. This particular C-17 (S/N 02-1109) saw combat action in Iraq and Afghanistan. It was also the last US military cargo aircraft to leave Afghanistan from Kabul AFB, in August 2021, before the airport was taken over by the Taliban. *USAF photo by 2Lt. Margaret Burneske*

This C-17 aircraft is from the 97th Airlift Mobility Wing, 58th Airlift Squadron, based at Altus AFB, Oklahoma. The base was the second base to receive C-17 aircraft, beginning in 1996. *John Gourley*

A C-17 loadmaster from the 97th Airlift Wing is conducting a combat offload at Altus AFB in February 2015, in which cargo is dropped out while the C-17 aircraft is taxiing, while another C-17 is landing. *USAF photo by A1C Nathan Clark*

This C-17 aircraft is parked at the 305th Airlift Mobility Wing at joint base McGuire-Dix-Lakehurst, New Jersey, in May 2017. *USAF photo by MSgt. Mark C. Olsen*

A C-17 from the 305th Airlift Mobility Wing has landed at Little Rock AFB in Arkansas as part of an operation to move 150 of the wing's airmen from the impact of Hurricane Irene on the East Coast in 2011. *USAF photo by MSgt. Mark C. Olsen*

This C-17 aircraft from the 436th Airlift has just arrived from its home base at Dover AFB, landing at Long Island MacArthur Airport in May 2019, where it will perform transport duties for the maintenance support team for the USAF Thunderbirds during the Jones Beach Air Show event. This wing is known as the Eagle Wing. *Ken Neubeck*

A C-17 aircraft taxi in front of the control tower at Dover AFB in January 2013. From this view, a number of the top fuselage antennas can be seen. *USAF photo by David S. Tucker*

A large contingency of C-17 aircraft are in the air from the 437th Airlift Wing, which is from the joint base in Charleston, South Carolina, during Operation Crescent Reach in May 2015. *USAF photo by SSgt. Corey Hook*

A C-17 aircraft from the 437th Airlift Wing is on the tarmac at Charleston AFB, preparing to evacuate to Fort Campbell, Kentucky, to escape the impact of Hurricane Matthew in October 2016. The 14th, 15th, and 16th Airlift Squadrons make up the 437th Airlift Wing. *USAF photo by SSgt. Corey Hook*

C-17 aircraft from the 437th Airlift Wing are conducting a multiple-aircraft exercise in May 2015 as part of Operation Crescent Reach in 2015. Note the skid marks on the runway from the multiple short landings conducted by the C-17. *USAF photo by TSgt. Nathan Lipscomb*

The last C-17 aircraft to be delivered at the 437th Airlift Wing at Charleston took place in September 2013, just over twenty years after delivery of the first C-17 at this base. Note the open main landing-gear bays. *USAF photo by TSgt. Rasheen Douglas*

Active ANG C-17 Units

This C-17 aircraft from the 105th Airlift Wing, 137th Airlift Squadron, from Stewart ANG is flying over Long Island Sound as it prepares to land at Gabreski Airport in Westhampton, New York, in 2015 to deliver equipment. The squadron is part of the 105th Airlift Wing, with the base receiving its first C-17 in 2011, and currently has nine aircraft in service. *Ken Neubeck*

A C-17 aircraft is seen here at Stewart ANG undergoing maintenance in a specially designed maintenance building that allows the trademark high tail of the aircraft to be accommodated by leaving it outside the building. Note the special cutout inserted in the doors to the building, used to accommodate the tail. *Ken Neubeck*

A C-17 aircraft is flying along the North Carolina coast on the way to the 145th ANG AW at Charlotte, North Carolina, in April 2018, as part of the formal acceptance ceremony in which the base will be transitioning from C-130 aircraft to the C-17. *USAF ANG photo by TSgt. Julianne M. Showalter*

Here is the same C-17 aircraft during the acceptance ceremony of new C-17 aircraft at the Charlotte ANG base in April 2018. *USAF ANG*

This C-17 aircraft from the 204th Airlift Squadron, under the 154th Airlift Wing, is preparing to leave the joint airbase at Pearl Harbor–Hickam, Hawaii, on its way to Puerto Rico in October 2017, during Hurricane Maria relief efforts. A rainbow is in the background. *USAF photo by TSgt. Shane Cuomo*

A C-17 aircraft from the 204th Airlift Squadron, under the 154th Airlift Wing from the Hawaii ANG, is ready to pick up a jeep during training at Wheeler AFB Harbor in March 2014. *USAF photo by Capt. Richard Barker*

A C-17 from the 164th Airlift Wing, Tennessee Air National Guard, taxis on the ramp at Tallinn Airport, Estonia, on June 14, 2016. The C-17 brought High Mobility Artillery Rocket System vehicles and soldiers from the Tennessee Army National Guard to participate in the Saber Strike 16 exercise, a cooperative training exercise designed to improve coordination with other participating nations. *Minnesota National Guard photo by TSgt. Amy M. Lovgren*

A C-17 aircraft from the 164th Airlift Wing, based in Memphis, Tennessee, landing at Amari Airbase, Estonia, during Operation Sabre Strike in June 2015. *USAF photo by TSgt. Chris Schepers*

Airmen assigned to the 167th Airlift Wing, based in Martinsburg, West Virginia, leave a C-17 aircraft at Alpena Combat Readiness Training Center, Alpena, Michigan, in May 2019. *US ANG photo by TSgt. Jodie Witmer*

A C-17 Globemaster III operated by the 167th Airlift Wing is loaded with six generators and a Large Area Maintenance Shelter from the 635th Materiel Maintenance Squadron, based at Holloman Air Force Base, New Mexico, in October 2018. The C-17 delivered the equipment to Tyndall AFB, Florida, the following day to provide aid in the aftermath of Hurricane Michael. *US ANG photo by Senior MSgt. Emily Beightol-Deyerle*

This C-17 aircraft is one of eight C-17 aircraft that were transferred from the 3rd Wing to the 176th Airlift Wing during a transfer ceremony at Elmendorf-Richardson AFB, Alaska, in May 2017. *US ANG photo by SSgt. Edward Eagerton*

This C-17 aircraft is from the 176th Airlift Wing and 144th Airlift Squadron, from the ANG unit in Elmendorf-Richardson Joint AFB, Alaska. It is participating in the Arctic Thunder Open House in June 2018. *USAF photo by Alejandro Pena*

An Air National Guard C-17 from the 183rd Airlift Squadron, assigned to the 172nd Airlift Wing (based in Jackson, Mississippi), has just taken off from Patrick AFB, Florida. *John Gourley*

A C-17 from the 183rd Airlift Squadron from the ANG unit based in Jackson is on deployment to Buckley AFB, Colorado, in 2016. This is one of nine C-17 aircraft that is assigned to the ANG base. *USAF photo by A1C Luke W. Nowakowski*

This C-17 aircraft is used by both the 60th AMW and the 349th AF Reserve Wing, which is based out of Travis AFB, California, with support personnel and pilots coming from both wings. This aircraft, "Spirit of Solano," bears the markings of both squadrons and is the first aircraft that was assigned to this squadron in 2006. *USAF photo by TSgt. Traci Keller*

The "Spirit of Solano" C-17 aircraft has just landed at MacArthur Airport in Long Island, New York, in May 2021, to support the Thunderbirds trip there. This aircraft has made many trips into different areas of the United States during its service. *Ken Neubeck*

CHAPTER 6

Foreign Sales

The C-17 has been ordered by seven different NATO countries as well as for the Strategic Airlift Capability (SAC) Program. Orders of this aircraft by different countries have permitted the production line to extend for an additional three years into 2015, which has allowed for the program to go past the initial USAF production order.

The Royal Air Force of the UK was the first country outside the US to receive a C-17. This aircraft was assigned RAF number ZZ171 and was delivered to the RAF in May 2001. The RAF would receive three additional C-17s in the first half of 2001.

The last seven C-17 aircraft off the production line were foreign sales, with Canada receiving one aircraft, the United Arab Emirates (UAE) receiving two, and Qatar receiving four. The last production C-17 was delivered to Qatar in the first half of 2016. The line would be closed despite various efforts by the company to pursue additional sales.

C-17 Foreign Military Sales Summary

Country	Quantity
India	10
UK (RAF)	8
Qatar	8
UAE	8
Australia (RAAF)	6
Canada	5
NATO (SAC)	3
Kuwait	2
TOTAL	50

Flight crew and maintenance crew from three different countries—United States, England, and Australia—assemble in front of their C-17 aircraft at open hours at RAF Brize Norton in the UK in June 2007. The RAF aircraft in the rear, serial number A41-206, was the first C-17 delivered to Australia, whereas the RAF aircraft in the foreground, serial number ZZ171, was the first C-17 delivered to England. *USAF photo by MSgt. Wendy Weidenhamer*

This Royal Australian Air Force (RAAF) C-17 from No. 36 Squadron is taxiing at the USAF base in Yokoda, Japan, in March 2011, during relief efforts to Japan. The tail marking shows a horse that comes from the RAAF emblem. *USAF photo by SSgt. Robin Stanshak*

An RAAF C-17 Globemaster III aircraft is being loaded with equipment during Operation Tomodachi at the USAF base in Yokoda, Japan, in March 2011, where assistance was provided to support Japan during disaster relief following the 2011 Tōhoku earthquake and tsunami. The RAAF operates eight C-17s from RAAF Base Amberley, Queensland. *USAF photo by A1C Andrea Salazar*

The UK has procured a total of five C-17 Globemaster III aircraft, which are operated by the RAF's No. 99 Squadron. This C-17 is at RAF Brize Norton in August 2010. *RAF photo by RAF A1C Tiffany Deuel / UK open government license*

No. 99 Squadron C-17 at RAF Brize Norton, England, is pictured en route to a flyover at Buckingham Palace for Queen Elizabeth's birthday in May 2002. *RAF photo by Sgt. Jack Prichard, DCC / UK open government license*

Col. Keith Boon, heavy-airlift commander, is in front of a C-17 based at Papa Air Base, Hungary, that is assigned to the Strategic Airlift Capability Program, which is supported by twelve different countries. *USAF photo by TSgt. Bennie J. Davis III*

A Qatar Emiri Air Force (QEAF) C-17 releases flares over a drop zone during joint US-Qatar exercises at Al-Qalael in Qatar. These exercises are part of the effort against the Islamic State of Iraq (ISIS) in the region. *USAF photo by SSgt. Corey Hook*

A QEAF C-17 Globemaster performs an airdrop during the Lahoub exercise at Al-Qalael drop zone in Qatar on May 9, 2018. The QEAF recently sent one of their C-17 aircrews back to the US to receive airdrop training. This is the first C-17 airdrop performed on the Gulf coast. *USAF photo by SSgt. Corey Hook*

A Royal Canadian Air Force C-17 and two C-130J Super Hercules aircraft from the 9th Wing Canadian Forces Base out of Trenton, Ontario, are parked at Thule Air Base, Greenland, in April 2014. The aircraft have brought fuel and other supplies for the Canadian forces stationed there, to get them through the harsh winter. *USAF photo by TSgt. David Buchanan*

This is the first Indian air force C-17 undergoing testing at Edwards AFB in January 2013, as conducted by the 418th Flight Test Squadron. India operates eleven C-17 aircraft in their air force. *USAF photo by Jet Fabara*

This is a C-17 that is operated by the United Arab Emirates (UAE), during landing in July 2011. The UAE has eight C-17 aircraft in their fleet. *Boeing*

This is the first of two C-17 aircraft that were transferred to Kuwait at Charleston AFB in February 2014. *USAF photo by SrA Dennis Sloan*

Five members of the Kuwait air force leave from the crew door of the first Kuwaiti C-17 aircraft, in February 2014. The team received training by being embedded with the 17th Airlift Squadron for the month of January. *USAF photo by SrA Dennis Sloan*

CHAPTER 7

Combat Operations: Operation Allied Force

For over twenty years, the C-17 has been an active part of USAF combat activities in different war theaters. The first combat-related activity for the C-17 took place in the Republic of Kosovo in 1998.

Operation Allied Force would be the first significant C-17 combat action. Twelve aircraft would be deployed, joining other USAF transport aircraft such as the C-130. The C-17 fleet of twelve flew up to twenty-two sorties a day and met supplied departure rates that were above peacetime averages.

The performance of the Air Force's C-17A airlifters was one of the great success stories of Operation Allied Force, since the aircraft flew half the strategic airlift missions required during the operation. Its capability to land on small and unimproved airfields, as well as its ability to rapidly offload cargo, was particularly important.

After the surrender of Serbian forces in the region, the C-17 fleet would see significant action in the movement of personnel and cargo. To support Task Force Falcon, conducted by the US Army, there would be 253 C-17 missions that moved 2,500 passengers and 12, 000 tons of cargo. The C-17 would first move troops from Ramstein, Germany, to Skopje, Macedonia, and then to Tirana, Albania, to collect soldiers who participated in Task Force Hawk. These soldiers were returned by the aircraft to either Ramstein or Skopje. The length of these missions required aerial refueling. The C-17 was a key part of the final peacekeeping phase of this war.

A C-17 Globemaster III aircraft from the 437th Airlift Wing, Charleston AFB, South Carolina, prepares to depart from Ramstein Air Base in Germany for Tirana, Albania, to provide relief supplies to the Kosovo refugees at the Albanian and Macedonian borders in support of Operation Sustain Hope in April 1999. *USAF photo by SSgt. Elfrain Gonzales*

A pair of C-17 Globemaster III aircraft from the 437 Airlift Wing, Charleston AFB, South Carolina, have landed on the wet runway at Rinas Airport in Tirana, Albania, from Ramstein Air Base, Germany, to provide relief supplies to the Kosovo refugees displaced from Albania and Macedonia, in support of Operation Sustain Hope in April 1999. *USAF photo by SSgt. Chris Steffen*

This bird's-eye view of the C-17 Globemaster III aircraft at Tirana, Albania, shows the massive amounts of supplies that have been dropped off from the aircraft during Operation Sustain Hope in April 1999. The C-17 would fly many such humanitarian missions during the war. *USAF photo by SSgt. Chris Steffen*

CHAPTER 8

Combat Operations: Operation Enduring Freedom

The C-17 would next see action during Operation Enduring Freedom, conducted in Afghanistan, with the extensive transport of troops and equipment beginning in late 2001.

Challenges that were faced during this operation included that large bases in the country—located in Kandahar and Bagram—had to be captured from enemy forces and then repaired after the effects of US bombing before they could be reopened for airlift operations. The C-17 could land at smaller airfields that were not as developed, but typically there would be no refueling capabilities at those fields. Thus, the aircraft had to carry more fuel, which limited total cargo loads, as well as relying more on aerial refueling. Additionally, during the early stages of the war, C-17s would leave their engines running when unloading cargo.

During the immediate period of the war from October 9 through November 7 of that year, seventy-eight C-17s flew over the Black Sea between Europe and Afghanistan to conduct this mission. From October through mid-December, many C-17 aircraft had to fly over the drop zone in the region at night only, and at altitudes above 25,000 feet due to the threat of enemy missiles. This situation affected the accuracy of the drops and possible damage to the cargo. In addition, the loadmasters had to wear oxygen masks and be subjected to cold temperatures when the cargo bay door was opened at these high altitudes.

The C-17 would be pressed into major evacuation duties during the evacuation of US personnel and Afghanistan citizens during the US exit from Afghanistan from Kabul Airport in August 2021. As many as thirty C-17 aircraft were used in this operation, with aircraft from several US bases and some other countries such as the UAE and Australia running daily flights. Over 123,000 people were evacuated.

The C-17 continues to be active in the different areas of the Middle East region where US personnel may be stationed in different operations. Missions include military deterrent operations and humanitarian missions; details of some of these missions are provided in this chapter.

A C-17 aircraft at Kandahar International Airport in Afghanistan during Operation Enduring Freedom in January 2002. The C-17 would face many challenges during this war, such as landing on remote and unimproved airfields. *USAF photo by Capt. Charles G. Grow.*

A C-17 aircraft lands in Incirlik Air Base in Turkey after conducting a support mission for Operation Enduring Freedom in Afghanistan in October 2001. The C-17 would fly missions from many different air bases in the Asian area during the beginning of combat operations in Afghanistan. *USAF photo by SrA Matthew Hannen*

This C-17 aircraft is taxiing to a parking spot at Karshi-Khanabad Air Base in Uzbekistan, with the aid of a US Army vehicle in support of Operation Enduring Freedom in March 2005. *USAF photo by MSgt. Scott T. Sturkol*

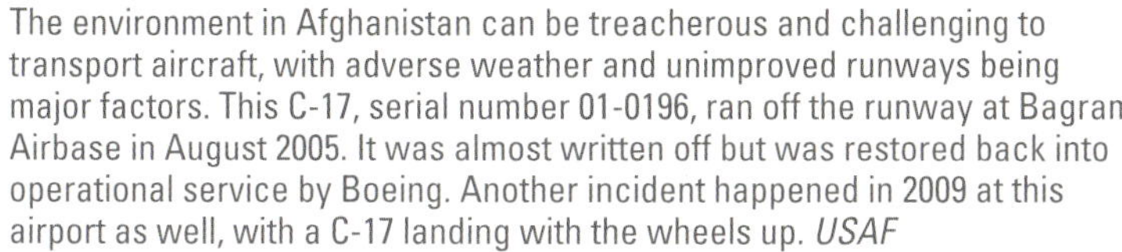

The environment in Afghanistan can be treacherous and challenging to transport aircraft, with adverse weather and unimproved runways being major factors. This C-17, serial number 01-0196, ran off the runway at Bagram Airbase in August 2005. It was almost written off but was restored back into operational service by Boeing. Another incident happened in 2009 at this airport as well, with a C-17 landing with the wheels up. *USAF*

Army vehicles pull the C-17 Globemaster from its location to the staging area on Forward Operating Base Shank, located in Logar Province of eastern Afghanistan. The aircraft ran off the runway in April 2012, due to inclement weather and freezing during the winter months. The aircraft was able to be flown back to America, where it was reconstructed and reintegrated into the Air Force fleet. *US Army photo by Sgt. Victor Everhart Jr.*

This C-17 aircraft from McChord AFB is being loaded with meal rations by the ground crew at Kandahar Airport in February 2002. *USAF photo by PH1 Ted Banks*

In August 2003, a C-17 aircraft has just landed at Bagram Air Base, while another is in the distance by the mountains. *USAF photo by Maj. Dave Honchul*

A C-17 aircraft delivers US Navy Sea Bees into Helmand Province of Afghanistan in March 2009, to aid in combat operations there. *US Navy photo by MCS 2nd Class Patrick W. Mullen*

C-17 loadmasters conduct an airdrop of supplies from the back end of the aircraft to forces below, over the southern region of Afghanistan in September 2009. *USAF photo by SSgt. Shawn Weismiller*

A C-17 aircraft delivers a US Marine Corps M1A2 Abrams Main Battle Tank (MBT) at Camp Bastion, Afghanistan, in November 2010, the first of seventeen M1AI tanks being delivered. This shipment marked the first time that US-owned tanks have been deployed in Afghanistan. *US Marine Corps photo by LCpl. McKenzie James*

A C-17 aircraft flies off near the mountains at Bagram Air Base in October 2014. C-130 aircraft are also seen at this base, likewise providing transport support. *USAF photo by SSgt. Evelyn Chavez*

The C-17 would be instrumental in the evacuation of people during the US withdrawal from Afghanistan in August 2021. Over thirty C-17s from several different US bases, as well as some from other countries such as the UAE and Australia, would be deployed in this operation in which 123,000 people were evacuated from Afghanistan to other countries. Here is a C-17 aircraft from the UAE in the process of evacuating people. *USAF photo by Sgt. Samuel Ruiz*

By August 2021, C-17 aircraft were not only moving US military personnel from Afghanistan, but also Afghan citizens to other countries. On August 15, 2021, a total of 640 Afghan citizens were transported in the cargo hold area of this C-17 aircraft deployed from Dover AFB, during evacuations of people who would be flown from Kabul to Qater. This is believed to be the most people ever flown in the C-17 aircraft. Large-scale operations like this continued until August 31, 2021. *USAF*

CHAPTER 9

Combat Operations: Operation Iraqi Freedom

When Operation Iraqi Freedom began in March 2003, C-17 aircraft were used to drop nearly 1,000 paratroopers of the 173rd Airborne Brigade onto Bashur airfield near Erbil in northern Iraq. This was the first time that the C-17 was used to support a combat airdrop, and this mission happened this way because Turkey would not allow USAF to use its bases to deliver troops and supplies into northern Iraq, and paratroopers were needed to secure this area.

One notable transport operation took place in March 2003, when a fleet of C-17s from the 62nd Airlift Wing delivered a full US Army brigade based in Aviano Air Base, Italy, into northern Iraq. Over the course of sixty-two airlift missions over five nights, C-17s delivered more than 400 vehicles, 2,000 personnel, and 3,000 tons of equipment without mishap.

Operations in Iraq would be curtailed in December 2011, with US troops being withdrawn from the region, with the help of C-17 transport. However, with the Iraqi government becoming unstable and the rise of ISIS in the region, US troops would be pulled back into the region a few years later.

The C-17 aircraft continues to be active in the different areas in the Middle East region where US military personnel are stationed in combat action against ISIS and other insurgents. Missions include both military and humanitarian missions; details on these operations are provided in this chapter.

US personnel deploy from a 437th Airlift Wing (Charleston AFB) C-17 at a forward base during Operation Iraqi Freedom in March 2003. *USAF photo by MSgt. Mark Bucher*

US Army paratroopers and USAF tactical air controllers from the 173rd Airborne Brigade board a C-17 aircraft on March 26, 2003, which will take them from an air base in Europe to participate in Operation Iraqi Freedom. *USAF photo by TSgt. Stephen Faulisi*

On March 26, 2003, a fleet of C-17 aircraft were used to transport 1,000 soldiers from the 173rd Airborne Brigade into the Kurdish-controlled area of northern Iraq in support of Operation Iraqi Freedom. This marked the first time that the aircraft was used in a combat airdrop. *USAF photo by TSgt. Stephen Faulisi*

Airmen from the 409th Air Expeditionary Group are deployed to Camp Sarafovo, Bulgaria, to palletize and load cargo for humanitarian aid onto a C-17 from McChord AFB in April 2003. The C-17 landed at Burgas Airport on its way to deliver aid to the people of Iraq. *USAF photo by MSgt. Dave Ahlschwede*

Ground crews load an Abrams tank onto a C-17 aircraft from the 17th Airlift Squadron at Ramstein Air Base, Germany, for delivery to Bashur Airfield, Iraq, in April 2003. *USAF photo by MSgt. Keith Reid*

This C-17 aircraft is on the parking ramp at Balad Air Base in Iraq in July 2006, after completing a mission supporting Operation Iraqi Freedom. *USAF photo by A1C Andrew Oquendo*

A C-17 aircraft from McGuire AFB lands at Balad Air Base in central Iraq in January 2008. *USAF photo by MSgt. John Nimmo Sr.*

A C-17 aircraft from McGuire AFB lands in a forward base in Southwest Asia in support of Operation Iraqi Freedom in October 2008. *USAF photo by A1C Jason Epley*

The C-17 was involved with significant amounts of troop transport during Operation Iraqi Freedom. Members of the 407th Air Expeditionary Group are leaving Ali Air Base on December 18, 2011; they were the last servicemen to leave Iraq at the time. *USAF photo by MSgt. Cecillo Ricardo*

However, subsequent action in the region required the C-17 to be involved in additional activities in Iraq. Here is a C-17 from McChord AFB that is involved in a humanitarian mission in Iraq in August 2014. *USAF photo by SSgt. Vernon Young Jr.*

Here is a C-17 that is parked on the runway at Sather Air Base in Iraq during a dust storm in April 2015. Visibility was reduced to 100 meters, and all air traffic was stopped. *USAF photo by TSgt. Jeffrey Allen*

A C-17 is landing while an F-16 is preparing for takeoff at Ballad Air Base in Iraq in October 2015. Hazy conditions due to dust are a hazard that aircrew have to deal with in this environment. *USAF photo by MSgt. John E. Laskey*

Air Force captains fly a C-17 at night from Iraqi Kurdistan in April 2016, after a review of the area by US officials to assess the campaign against ISIS. The war activity had moved against ISIS forces in northern Iraq and Syria in 2016 and became Operation Inherent Resolve. *DOD photo by Petty Officer 2nd Class Dominique A. Pineiro, US Navy*

As war action moved toward the area of northern Iraq and Syria, C-17 aircraft would be used for numerous transport missions for Operation Inherent Resolve. A loadmaster from the 816th Expeditionary Airlift Squadron marshals a vehicle onto the C-17 during combat airlift operations for US and coalition forces in Iraq and Syria in November 2017. *USAF photo by TSgt. Gregory Brook*

CHAPTER 10

Special Missions

The C-17 aircraft is often seen in public, not only for military transport but when the aircraft is pressed into special duties that are not related to military functions. These include support missions for transporting personnel to remote locations, such as for scientific studies.

The C-17 shares transport duties with the C-130 Hercules in support of the USAF Thunderbirds aerobatic team each year. Unlike the setup that the Blue Angels aerobatic team uses where a permanent C-130 known as Fat Albert is assigned to the team on a full-time basis, the C-17 aircraft is temporarily assigned to the Thunderbirds, depending on the nearest USAF base with transport aircraft. Thus, the C-17 will carry both equipment and personnel, drop these off prior to an air show event, and then come a few days later to collect the same.

As illustrated in this chapter, there are many nonmilitary missions where C-17 has been pressed into emergency duties at various times. This includes transport missions for transporting food supplies and medicine to impacted areas around the world, as well as support for areas that have been struck by natural disasters such as earthquakes and tsunamis. Additionally, the C-17 is used to support scientific missions conducted at the South Pole, leading to certain challenges.

The most sensitive mission that the aircraft has flown was the August 2018 transfer of war remains of US servicemen who died in the Korean War (1950–53).

As cited previously in this book, dozens of C-17s were used in the massive evacuation of service and civilian personnel from Afghanistan during August 2021, in which 123,000 people were airlifted.

The C-17 aircraft is used regularly to support the USAF Thunderbirds aerobatic team. Here a C-17 from Charleston AFB is being unloaded with equipment to support the Thunderbirds during a visit to Republic Airport in May 2007, during the team's air show event at Jones Beach in Long Island. *Lynn McDonald / LIRAHS*

Personnel depart from a C-17 from McChord AFB, Washington, in August 2007, at Pegasus White Ice Runway, Antarctica, during an Operation Deep Freeze winter fly-in mission. *USAF photo by TSgt. Shane A. Cuomo*

A C-17 from McChord AFB is parked on the runway at McMurdo Station in Antarctica in November 2011 as part of Operation Deep Freeze, where the aircraft provides airlift support to the National Science Foundation. During this particular visit, the temperature reached a high of 20°F to a low of –35°F. *USAF*

The mission to McMurdo continues to the present day. Here a McChord AFB C-17 is shown bringing personnel to the base in November 2018. *USAF photo by SMSgt. Joseph Carter*

A pallet sled is used to unload cargo from a C-17 aircraft from McChord AFB in August 2007 at Pegasus White Ice Runway, Antarctica, during an Operation Deep Freeze winter fly-in mission. The aircraft brings scientists, support personnel, food, and equipment for the US Antarctic Program at McMurdo Station, Antarctica. *USAF photo by TSgt. Shane A. Cuomo*

Maintenance personnel are using portable heater units to warm up the engines of a C-17 aircraft at McMurdo Station, Antarctica, prior to engine start in the cold climate. *USAF photo by TSgt. Shane A. Cuomo*

A C-17 carries members of the US Agency for International Development (USAID) elite disaster team, along with equipment out of Travis AFB, California, to go to Mexico to help in search and rescue after a 7.1-magnitude earthquake struck the country on September 21, 2017. The team consists of the Los Angeles County Fire Department Urban search-and-rescue team, which had previously flown on USAF transport aircraft such as the C-17. *USAF photo by MSgt. Joseph Swafford*

A C-17 arrives in Mexico City on September 21, 2017, with the members of the US Agency for International Development elite disaster team, to help in the search-and-rescue efforts. *USAF photo by MSgt. Joseph Swafford*

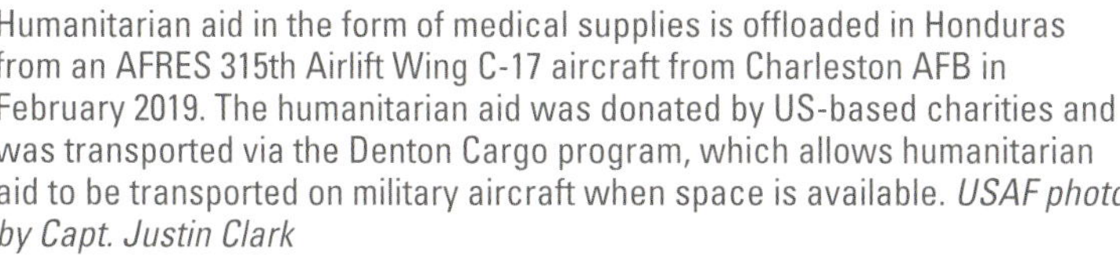

Humanitarian aid in the form of medical supplies is offloaded in Honduras from an AFRES 315th Airlift Wing C-17 aircraft from Charleston AFB in February 2019. The humanitarian aid was donated by US-based charities and was transported via the Denton Cargo program, which allows humanitarian aid to be transported on military aircraft when space is available. *USAF photo by Capt. Justin Clark*

The C-17 is used to transport equipment in different areas of the world where military and peacekeeping activity is taking place. Here is a UH-60 Blackhawk helicopter from the Multinational Force and Observers (MFO) being loaded into a C-17 aircraft from the 62nd Air Wing in the Sinai Peninsula in Egypt in 2014. The helicopter is being transported to Germany for significant maintenance. *US Army photo by Sgt. Thomas Duval*

A C-17 Globemaster III delivers humanitarian aid from Homestead Air Reserve Base, Florida, to Cucuta, Colombia, on February 16, 2019. This mission was conducted as requested by the US secretary of state, in close coordination with USAID and with the approval of the government of Colombia. Urgently needed aid was sent to Colombia for eventual distribution by relief organizations on the ground for Venezuelans impacted by the crisis in their country. *USAF photo by TSgt. Gregory Brook*

US personnel load the UH-60 Blackhawk helicopter from the MFO (with emblem on nose) into the cargo area of the C-17. *US Army photo by Sgt. Thomas Duval*

A C-17 aircraft leaves Osan Air Base, South Korea, on August 1, 2018, on a solemn mission in carrying fifty-five transfer cases that contain the remains of US servicemen from the Korean War, through an agreement made between the US and North Korea. The aircraft is headed for Hickam AFB, Hawaii, for a ceremony and for the US Defense Department to identify the remains. *USAF photo by SrA Kelsey Tucker*

In the cargo area of the C-17 are the transfer cases containing the remains of fifty-five US servicemen from the Korean War, after the aircraft's arrival at Hickam AFB on August 2, 2018. The remains will be processed by US experts for identification. *USAF photo by SrA Apryl Hall*

The remains of missing US service personnel from the Korean War, contained in US flag-draped coffins, are carried by US honor guards during a solemn ceremony in the ramp area of the cargo of the two C-17 aircraft at Pearl Harbor–Hickam AFB in August 2018. *USAF photo by SrA Apryl Hall*

On August 28, 2021, US personnel are shown loading a CH-47 Chinook helicopter onto a Travis AFB C-17 during removal of US military equipment from Kabul Airport, Afghanistan. *US Army photo*

A pair of C-17s are shown arriving at Al Salem AB, Kuwait, in August 2021, carrying evacuees from Afghanistan. The two aircraft are from Martinsburg ANG and Mississippi ANG and were part of the dozens of C-17s from various US bases used during the evacuation. *USAF photo by TSgt. Daryn Murphy*

Soldiers from the Minnesota ANG are loaded into the C-17 cargo hold after completing their mission in Afghanistan and are on the way to Al Salem AB, Kuwait, on August 17, 2021. *US Army photo by Cpl. Bridget Haugh*

Nighttime evacuation takes place on August 21, 2021, at Kabul Airport in Afghanistan, with evacuees entering a C-17 aircraft from Dover AFB. *USAF photo by SA Taylor Crul*

A C-17 releases defensive flares during a flight in May 2006. Defensive flares are used to protect the aircraft against ground fire when flying over high-risk areas. *USAF photo by TSgt. Russell E. Cooley*

AIR FORCE
0223
AMC
CHARLESTON
USAF